...D
PRINCE EDWARD
ISLAND
ADVENTURE AND
LIGHTHOUSE GUIDE

DAVE STEPHENS AND SUSAN RANDLES

NIMBUS
PUBLISHING LTD

Nimbus Publishing Limited
PO Box 9301, Station A
Halifax, NS B3K 5N5
(902) 455-4286

Design: Arthur Carter
Cover Photo: Dave Stephens
Photo Credits: Dave Stephens
Printed and bound in Canada

Canadian Cataloguing in Publication Data
Stephens, David E., 1946-
Discover Prince Edward Island: Adventure and Lighthouse Guide
ISBN 1-55109-280-8
1. Prince Edward Island—Guidebooks. I. Randles, Susan, 1958-
II. Title.
FC2607.S73 1998   917.1704'4   C98-950273-2
F1047.S73 1998

Nimbus Publishing acknowledges the financial support of the Canada Council and the Canadian Department of Heritage.

To Evan, Julia, Patsy, and Hilarey, with love.

Contents

Acknowledgements

There are four special people who assisted in the preparation of this guidebook and whose comments are noted in quotes throughout the book: Pasty Cox (P.C.) and Hilarey ("Penny") Davis (P.D.). Both assisted in the collection of material, and we sincerely thank them. Our son, Evan Randles Hahn (E.R.H.) (age twelve), and our niece, Julia Cox (J.C.) (age fifteen), spent over a week touring Prince Edward Island from one end to the other. They assisted in navigation, participated in and commented on activities, collected information, and appeared in a number of photographs. We appreciate their eager cooperation, which helped make this project enjoyable and successful.

Thanks to Carol Horne, Manager of Advertising and Publicity at Tourism PEI, for her support and advice, as well as to Laura Hagen, Familiarization Tour Officer. Lyanne Love at the PEI Museum and Heritage Foundation, and Parks Program Supervisor Kevin MacLaren at PEI Provincial Parks provided helpful advice and information. We extend our gratitude to Carol Livingstone of the PEI Lighthouse Society and Bev Cleveland at the Canadian Coast Guard in Charlottetown for their advice and to Noel Palmer, retired from the Coast Guard service, who provided historical information. We especially thank George Craig, who works for the Canadian Coast Guard in Charlottetown. He was kind enough to share with us his detailed listing of light stations and range lights to cross-reference with our research and ensure an accurate and complete lighthouse guide. Without the cooperation of the owners and operators of the properties we visited, we could not have completed this book.

We thank Andrea, Julie and the other very capable staff members at Walmart One Hour Photo Lab (Penhorn Mall, Dartmouth, NS) for their quality processing and friendy attitude.

Finally, we wish to express our appreciation to Dorothy Blythe, publisher at Nimbus, for her suggestions and guidance from the inception of this project to finished text. As always, the editorial and design staff have made our work seem easier.

Introduction

To discover the nooks and crannies of Prince Edward Island's beautiful countryside is to discover an enchanting medley of rich colour, where verdant patchwork fields stretch out beneath an endless cobalt sky to meet the surrounding sea. Prince Edward Island is a photographer's dream come true: magnificent sunsets, refreshing open spaces, and pastoral settings await. Distinctive red headlands, white sandy beaches, and a changeable, sculpted coastline are part of what endear the Island to those who visit time and again.

Prince Edward Island is unique in North America. At 5,660 sq. km (2,185 sq. mi.), it is Canada's smallest province. Yet, over a million visitors a year come to enjoy the natural beauty, pristine beaches, and warm hospitality of the Island's 130,000 or so residents. What many people discover is a laid-back, slower paced Island lifestyle, which entices them to return again and again. The Island is much smaller than many people realize from a glance at a provincial road map (about 195 km or 121 mi. long and 65 km or 40 mi. wide); therefore, distances can be deceiving. But the accessible size is part of the Island's appeal.

At first, some visitors are a little frustrated when they encounter farm equipment moving slowly along side roads or two cars delaying traffic for a few moments while the drivers exchange greetings in front of a local post office. It usually takes a day or two for those "from away" to realize that gearing down to enjoy life is one of the reasons they came to Prince Edward Island in the first place. Driving on the Island requires one to slow down and relax; the breathtaking scenery is endless and there's so much to explore, visitors simply can't hurry past. The major highways, including the Trans-Canada, are mostly two lanes from which driveways veer off in all directions. Adjusting to the "Island way of life" allows visitors to appreciate the spirit of the province that is characterized by its landscape, its geographical location—between the Northumberland Strait and the Gulf of St. Lawrence—its history, cultures, and heritage.

Although we have frequently visited Prince Edward Island for many years, the preparation of this book gave us an excuse to explore new places that had escaped our attention on previous journeys. Visitors will find an array of friendly, often unique establishments that will provide enjoyment and entertainment. On the Island, almost every attraction or property one could visit is family owned and operated. Regardless of how commercial an establishment might be, visitors will be struck by the genuine hospitality and irrepressible charm that are signatures of Prince Edward Island. Islanders' obvious pride in their businesses and homes is reflected in well-kept, well-run properties.

Visitors should bear in mind that July and August are the high season, and it is advisable to book accommodations well in advance to obtain the type and location you desire. However, last minute bookings are possible by calling 1-888-268-6667 for accommodation vacancy information.

A note about the contents: This guidebook is divided into the six familiar DayTour regions established in the provincial Visitors Guide (available from Prince Edward Island Tourism at Visitor Information Centres throughout the province or by requesting a copy from Tourism PEI, Box 940, Charlottetown, PE, C1A 7M5 or e-mail tourpei@gov.pe.ca or calling 1-888-734-7529). Within each region, we have selected "adventure" sites and lighthouses, which we believe visitors will find particularly interesting or are representative of what the Island has to offer.

The adventures illustrate the wide array of activities located throughout the province. Unfortunately, many people equate Cavendish with Prince Edward Island. While the Cavendish area has received a vast amount of publicity over the years, and it does have a plethora of commercial attractions, visitors wishing to fully experience the Island should also go farther afield. Accommodations in other areas are often easier to book and may even be more economical. By moving beyond the summertime tourist areas, visitors will be rewarded with greater insight into the true character and beauty of Prince Edward Island and those that call the fair isle home.

Some activities and adventures described in this book apply to a particular site; others, such as deep-sea fishing or trail riding, may be found throughout the Island, and we have personally selected a representative operation or property to describe. This should not be taken as a recommendation or any indication that one operation is superior to another.

Most seasonal operations are open from May to

October, although these periods vary greatly with individual operations. During the shoulder periods, before July and after August, the days and times of operation may be reduced. Visitors are advised to call ahead for current details regarding such changeable information as hours of operation, prices, and amenities.

The other dimension to this guide is a listing of lighthouses within the DayTour regions. Lighthouses have played an important role in the seafaring life of Prince Edward Island from the "first generation" lighthouses (octagon shape, built before 1873) to the "second generation" lights (square, tapered, built after 1873). With modern technology (including the use of fibreglass and metal), many of these former "signposts of the sea" are disappearing. However, considerable effort has been made to not only preserve as many lighthouses and range lights as possible but make them accessible to the public. "Lighthouse hunting" can result in viewing some of the most beautiful and "undiscovered" scenery on the Island.

The Prince Edward Island Lighthouse Society has worked towards preserving these beacons for future generations. A folder on lighthouses and an activity sheet are available from Visitor Information Centres or from lighthouses open to the public. Information plaques have been mounted on fifteen of the most prominent light stations (indicated in the Lighthouses sections with an asterisk, *), and visitors who collect at least eight "brass rubbings" ("rubbings" may be obtained by laying the activity sheet over a small square relief drawing on each plaque and rubbing the sheet with a pencil or pen) will be awarded a Lighthouse Lovers certificate. (A membership fee of twenty-five dollars provides three issues of the society's newsletter. Contact Carol Livingstone, RR # 2, O'Leary, PEI, C0B 1V0; tel./fax (902)859-3117.)

We have endeavoured to provide information about and directions to reach most of the traditional lighthouses and range lights (two lights positioned apart to guide vessels into a harbour); however, lights may be decommissioned and removed at any time. We did not include the light on St. Peters Island (it's not visible from the mainland); the structure at the Canadian Coast Guard facilities in Charlottetown (built for decorative purposes); privately built light towers used as cottages, homes or tourist attractions, and therefore never an official light station; or skeleton towers, masts or other similar modern structures.

Caution: Lights were originally erected as navigational aids not as tourist attractions; therefore, visiting some light stations requires a reasonable degree of caution. Some lights are at the end of narrow, single-lane roads (most of which are very muddy in the spring or wet weather). Others are situated atop steep cliffs without protective fencing, or they may be located across private property (which should never be crossed without the owners' permission). Several lights are located near parallel breakwaters forming "runs" into a harbour resulting in extreme currents, which make swimming very dangerous. Many lights have automatic foghorns that are set off by sensors (it doesn't have to be foggy for the horn to sound), so visitors should keep clear of the foghorn systems to avoid any chance of hearing damage.

Key to Symbols

Free / $ to $$$$ Admission cost: Approximate fee for one adult. Most operations charge less or offer free admission for children, or they have a family rate. **Range: $** up to $5; **$$** up to $10; **$$$** up to $15; **$$$$** over $15. (Due to changes in pricing from one season to the next, this should be used only as a guide.)

Family activity: These adventures are appropriate for the whole family.

Rainy day activity: Many activities on the Island are outdoor-related, and a day of rain may reduce options. These activities or adventures are mainly indoors, although umbrellas or rain jackets on hand would be advisable.

Wheelchair accessible

Partly wheelchair accessible: Call ahead for details.

National Park or Historic Site

Provincial Park or Historic Site

Scenic Location: While most of Prince Edward Island is indeed beautiful, we have selected a few of our personal favourites that offer striking scenes or vistas.

Day Tour Areas
of Prince Edward Island

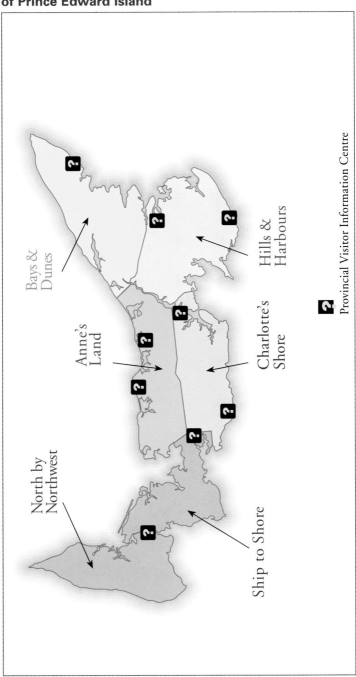

Provincial Visitor Information Centre

Hills &
Harbours

Bays &
Dunes

Anne's
Land

Charlotte's
Shore

North by
Northwest

Ship to Shore

Discover
Prince Edward Island
Adventure and
Lighthouse Guide

1. Hills & Harbours

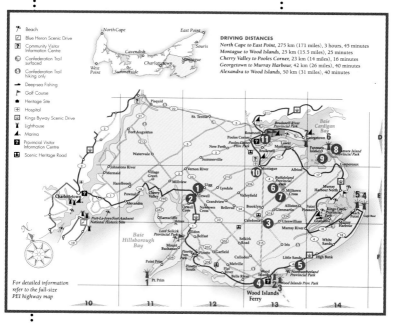

DRIVING DISTANCES
North Cape to East Point, 275 km (171 miles), 3 hours, 45 minutes
Montague to Wood Islands, 25 km (15.5 miles), 25 minutes
Cherry Valley to Pooles Corner, 23 km (14 miles), 16 minutes
Georgetown to Murray Harbour, 42 km (26 miles), 40 minutes
Alexandra to Wood Islands, 50 km (31 miles), 40 minutes

For detailed information refer to the full-size PEI highway map

● Adventures

1 Sir Andrew Macphail Homestead

2 Orwell Corner Historic Village

3 Moonsnail Soapworks and Aromatherapy

4 Northumberland Ferries Limited

5 Rossignol Estate Winery

6 Buffaloland Provincial Park

7 Harvey Moore Wildlife Management Area

8 Panmure Island Provincial Park

9 Clam Digging: Panmure Island

10 Cruise Manada

11 Brudenell Trail Rides

⍓ Lighthouses

1 Point Prim

2 Wood Islands

3 Wood Islands Harbour Range

4 Cape Bear

5 Murray Harbour Range

6 Panmure Head

7 Georgetown Range

Hills and Harbours: Introduction

The tranquil southeast region of Prince Edward Island encompasses portions of Kings and Queens Counties. The Scottish heritage of the region still predominates in lively ceilidhs (pronounced "kay-lees"- impromtu parties featuring traditional Celtic music) and historic sites, such as the Sir Andrew Macphail Homestead and Orwell Corner Historic Village. The Hills and Harbours area is aptly named, for the scenery here ranges from gently sloped farmland to some of the Island's best beaches—like the one at Panmure Island—to peaceful harbours around which tidy fishing villages

Watching the sun set at Murray Harbour.

are arranged. People travelling via Northumberland Ferries from Nova Scotia dock at the Wood Islands Ferry Terminal where they can travel to Charlotte-town on the Trans-Canada Highway or take a more leisurely jaunt, exploring the scenic southeast.

A number of lighthouses grace the shoreline of this region and capture part of the Maritime heritage that predominates the province. The Point Prim lighthouse, for instance, is the oldest on the Island. For those interested in cultural landmarks, they won't want to miss out on a chance to see some of the lights that overlook striking vistas and evoke a seafaring history.

Sir Andrew Macphail Homestead

Orwell is the birthplace of Sir Andrew Macphail (1864-1938), physician, professor, author, journalist, editor, and organizer of the Canadian Field Ambulance corps. His homestead—once a working farm—where he returned each summer and conducted agricultural experiments, was an important part of his life and environmental interests. Today it is a unique combination of natural and social history.

The house contains period furnishings and is open to the public. Community events are held here, from storytelling to Ceilidh nights. A fully licensed restaurant is operated in the former parlour/music room.

The 57-ha (140-acre) property features three nature trails ranging from the 87-m (95-yd.) Rhododendron Trail to the 1.5-km (0.9 mi.) Woodland Trail that extends through a forested area. (Better bring some insect repellent.) Native and non-native tree species inhabit the forest. Wildlife abounds in the form of birds, stream dwellers in the Orwell River, wildflowers, and small mammals.

During July an environmental education program provides an opportunity for children to "Share a Love of Nature" by exploring the surrounding flora and fauna. Other programs throughout the summer encourage everyone to participate in workshops, including walks that highlight tree and shrub identification, ferns, mushrooms, and other aspects of the nature trails that surround the homestead.

Adventure

Off Route 1, Orwell
tel. (902)651-2789
seasonal
www.isn.net/~dhunter
/macphailfoundation.
html

The Macphail Homestead opens a door to the past.

Free

Off the Trans-Canada
Highway at Orwell
tel. (902)651-2013 or
(off-season)
(902)368-6600
Seasonal
www.metamedia.pe.
ca/peimuseum

Open a door to the past at Orwell Corner Historic
Village. The buildings, which include a blacksmith
shop, general store, schoolhouse, church and farm
buildings have been here for over a century—from
the 1890s, when Orwell Corner was a small
agricultural community.

Apart from glimpses into a way of life that few
of us have experienced, the village presents a quiet
retreat where sprawling flower gardens create a tranquil atmosphere. Bring a picnic lunch and sit in the
cool shade of a tree. Enjoy a visit with the horses
beside the pasture fence. Explore the buildings and
talk to costumed guides to learn about a lifestyle
that makes many appreciate the conveniences of

Visitors can practice
forgotten trades.

our modern society.

Special events
and activities, such
as Wednesday
evening ceilidhs, a
horse weight pull,
Harvest Home
Festival, and
Victorian
Christmas Dinner,
are held on site.
Call for details and
schedules.

Orwell Corner is a
retreat into history
for all the family.

Moonsnail Soapworks and Aromatherapy

3

Moonsnail Soapworks and Aromatherapy is located in an old general store that hugs the road in the tiny village of Caledonia. At the storefront, teeming in heavenly aromas, are soap chips available as free samples and large blocks, which can be cut into bars at home as needed.

At the intersection of Routes 24 and 315; Tel. 1-888-771-SOAP; open all year by chance or appointment.

The soap is made from olive, coconut, and palm oils with herbs, spices, and pure essential oils for scent. At the back of the store, brother and sister team Jennifer and Gregory Ridgway use a creative

flair in crafting their soaps and natural body care products as well as aromatherapy blends. If you visit on a day when one of the small batches is under production, you may see how ingenuity has resulted in the creation not only of quality products but interesting soap-making equipment.

"A great variety of handmade natural soaps." J.C.

Buying handmade soaps is a treat for the senses.

Free

While the Confederation Bridge makes passage from New Brunswick to Prince Edward Island quick and easy, the Wood Islands to Caribou, Nova Scotia ferry is fortunately still in operation. A trip to the Island wouldn't be the same without the traditional ferry ride. The leisurely cruise to or from Prince Edward Island is in keeping with the relaxed "Island way of life" that so many visitors seek out and return to enjoy.

A mini cruise to the Island.

Transporting vehicles and foot passengers between Nova Scotia and Prince Edward Island about every two hours during the summer months, the large modern vessels complete the crossing in seventy-five minutes, just enough time to relax in the sun on the upper deck or take a stroll and let the salty sea breeze refresh your spirit.

The ferry company operates modern terminal facilities at both ends of the route. As with the Confederation Bridge, payment is made only when leaving Prince Edward Island. Many visitors arrive from New Brunswick via the Bridge, explore the Island, then take the ferry to Nova Scotia to complete a tour of the Maritimes. For schedules and fares call 1-888-249-SAIL.

Rossignol Estate Winery

Robert Louis Stevenson described wine as "bottled poetry." The Rossignol Estate Winery in Little Sands invites visitors to uncork some of that poetry while enjoying the serenity and beauty of a lush green vineyard.

Often referred to as Canada's only saltwater farm winery, it was established by the Rossignol family in 1995 along the picturesque south shore. Rows of grapevines are surrounded by rolling pastures dotted with grazing sheep. Using their own grapes or those purchased from others in the area, all of the wines are produced on site and include a number of red and white barrel-aged table wines. Local produce is also used to create a number of fruit wines such as strawberry-rhubarb and raspberry.

The winery has a capacity of forty-five thousand bottles. The labels for the wine bottles feature the talents of local artist Nancy Perkins as well as the owner/winemaker John Rossignol.

Tastings, available in the modern tasting room/gift shop, cost one dollar per ounce (all proceeds go to the local hospital). Informal tours are offered upon request to view the production area behind the tasting room.

Route 4, Little Sands; 9 km (6 mi.) east of Wood Islands ferry tel. (902)962-4193 Seasonal with reduced hours on Sunday

John Rossignol uncorks some poetry.

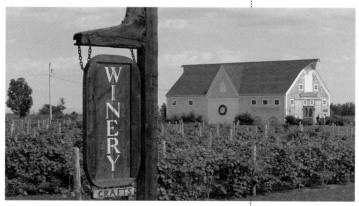

A tranquil stop along the way.

Free

Buffaloland Provincial Park

On Route 4, about
6 km (4 mi.) south of
Montague
tel. (902)652-2356
Open year-round

Prince Edward Island is probably the last place in Canada where one would expect to find two dozen buffalo roaming in a herd. But along Route 4, near Montague, buffalo do graze, along with white-tailed deer on 40 ha (100 acres) of pasture and forest. The original animals that comprised this herd were a gift to the province from the government of Alberta. On especially warm days, the herd stays close to the woods and may not be readily visible, even from the elevated viewing platform situated between two large fenced areas. The best time to see the herds is early in the morning, just after sunrise when the massive and, at one time, nearly extinct buffalo graze in the open. Dusk is another prime viewing time.

Where the buffalo
roam.

If the animals are grazing in the field nearest the highway, the best viewpoint may be from outside the high fence that encloses the area. Otherwise, drive into the park to walk along the pathway that leads to an elevated platform and information boards about the buffalo and deer. Picnic tables are provided to enjoy a packed lunch or just relax in the open fresh air.

Free

Harvey Moore Wildlife Management Area

In the same area of Buffaloland Provincial Park at Milltown Cross is the Harvey Moore Wildlife Management Area. A small narrow driveway leads into a large parking area, which often is shared by an array of ducks that seem to gather as if to welcome visitors. There are ample feathered creatures to feed and observe throughout the scenic area.

There are large display boards that highlight the life of founder Harvey Moore and the work he did to create this haven for migratory waterfowl. Through his efforts, Canada geese, blue geese, and black ducks have a safe sanctuary in the woods and ponds that Mr. Moore purchased to protect the avian creatures.

Route 4 in Milltown Cross
tel. (902)838-4834
Open seasonally from dawn to dusk

Bird-watchers will especially enjoy the nature trails that cover part of the natural bird habitat. Trout fishing is available at the back pond after July 1. Bring your own supplies.

A bird lover's paradise.

Free

On Route 347, north
of Gaspereaux
Services provided
seasonally
Campground tel.
(902)838-0668 or
(902)652-2356 (off-
season)
Rates apply to
campground.
Call for details.
Lighthouse open
seasonally

There are two beaches to enjoy at this park—one is
a sheltered bay beach, perfect for clam digging, the
other's white sandy shores meet the ocean, creating
a popular recreational area. Visitors to the park find
a swim hard to resist. Many will pull off onto the
side of the road, climb over the sand dunes, and
run into the inviting water. The sun warms small
pools, captured with the outgoing tide, transform-
ing them into natural hot tubs. In season, there is a
beach house open with change rooms and showers,
so there's really no excuse to pass up the temptation
to splash around in the soothing salt water.

The most magnificent view, from atop the
Panmure Island lighthouse, enables visitors to
appreciate the full length and depth of the beach
areas. When the light is open to the public, there
is a small admission charged: $2.50 adults, $1.25
children.

Island-hopping
without a boat.

"The vast expanse of sand, sea and sun was
beautiful. A pervasive sense of peace surrounding an
elderly couple in their lawn chairs on an otherwise
vacant beach watching the ocean, perhaps waiting
for the sunset." H.D.

Free

Clam digging

One of the Island's popular attractions is its delectable, fresh seafood. Not only can visitors enjoy such tasty molluscs as clams, they can have some fun harvesting a meal's worth themselves. Prime clam digging locations, such as the bay beach side of Panmure Island causeway, will be found throughout the province. Inquire locally for the best places.

To locate these buried molluscs, walk along the sand flats at low tide, carefully watching for the telltale squirt of water through small holes in the sand. By digging around these holes with a shovel, the clam can be readily retrieved—they aren't usually burrowed very deep beneath the surface.

Clam digging is fun for everyone.

Prepare the clams for cooking by scrubbing the shells (preferably with a brush) under running water then soak them up to an hour in salt water so they will expel any sand. Put the clams into a large covered pot (available in most rented cottages) with a small amount of water and steam over low to medium heat until the shells open (up to fifteen minutes). Don't overcook! Discard any shells that are broken or don't fully open. Remove the remaining clams to bowls or plates. Strain the broth to use for dipping. Melted butter with a touch of lemon juice (served in dishes with a little boiling water to keep the butter, which floats, hot) makes the clams even more delicious. Remove the meat from the shell by the black neck. (Some people remove the dark outer edge by simply sliding it off the neck.) Dip the meat in broth, then butter, and enjoy.

Free

Montague Marina
on Route 4 and
Brudenell Resort
Marina on Route 3
tel. 1-800-986-3444
Seasonal
www.peisland.com/
cruise/manada.htm

Seal-watching is a great way to learn about nature and the environment while taking a leisurely cruise. Seals, from pups to massive bulls, are fascinating creatures in their natural habitat.

The best seal-watching area is along the east end of the Island. For instance, there is Captain Garry's seal-watching operation out of Murray River (call 1-800-496-2494) and Capt. Dan Bears of Cruise Manada departs Montague and Brudenell in rain or shine. Passengers board fully equipped vessels that meet all the requirements for safety and comfort. The boats have washroom facilities, full canopy, and clear roll-down sides in the event of rain.

Taking a seal
cruise.

The Manada cruise is a couple of hours along the scenic Montague and Brudenell Rivers, which are branches of Georgetown Harbour. In addition to colonies of harbour seals, the tour passes by a mussel farm. Native seabirds and, occasionally, porpoises may be spotted. It's a good idea to bring binoculars to capture as much detail as possible. Reservations are recommended.

$$$$

Brudenell Trail Rides

Trail horses are usually gentle creatures that treat even novice riders with care. Fun for the whole family, a trail ride from one of a half dozen stables throughout Prince Edward Island can meander through a forest or field or along a beach.

At Brudenell Provincial Park, the trail rides cover all these settings and more. Thirty-minute or hour-long leisurely rides are accompanied by an experienced guide. Traverse green fields bordering the Brudenell River for an exhilarating sense of freedom or meander along the forest pathway to enjoy the scents and sounds of the serene woodland. When the tide is low the horses are directed along the beach, although most riders want to splash their mounts through the cool, shallow water. Reservations are recommended.

Brudenell
Provincial Park,
Route 3
tel. (902)652-2396
or (902)838-3713
(in winter)
Seasonal

"You don't need to feel intimidated." J.C.
"To be perched high on a horse in such magnificent settings is to experience pure elation." H.D.

Trail riding the
Island way.

  $$$

1 **Point Prim** *

Enjoy a beautiful drive out to Point Prim that passes through lush acres of potato fields neatly arranged in straight rows beneath an azure sky canopy. The tiny community of Point Prim and the lighthouse are situated at the end of a long narrow peninsula that juts into the Northumberland Strait. The oldest lighthouse on Prince Edward Island—erected in 1846—the Point Prim tower stands 18 m (60 ft.) tall, and the 46-cm (18-in.) walls are covered in wood shingles. The light was automated in 1969.

The operating light station was designed by Sir Isaac Smith in 1845 and is one of only two round brick lighthouses built in Canada.

Climbing to the top of the lighthouse takes a little effort, but the view beyond the green lawn and red rocky shoreline is worth the exertion. Take a break on the way up the steep steps and examine the artifacts and information presented for viewing.

The lighthouse is surrounded by wide lawns. There are picnic tables and a small play area for children. The stone beach is a bit rough but the layers of sandstone create tidal pools when the water is low, perfect for discovering sea creatures.

Welcome to
**Point Prim
Lighthouse**
• The oldest lighthouse on P.E.I.
• Built in 1845
• Designed by Sir Issac Smith
• Fully automated in 1969
• The only round brick lighthouse in Canada

**Guided tours available
July & August**

Point Prim, PEI's oldest lighthouse.

Directions: At the end of Route 209 (lane to the left), off the Trans-Canada Highway. Open July and August.

"A sense of safety and peace in the presence of such a solid, tall white structure with an omnipresent light." H. D.

Wood Islands *

Built in 1876 at a cost of five thousand dollars, this lovely square wooden tower is built into the end of the lightkeeper's house and sits majestically atop a red cliff overlooking the ferry terminal at Wood Islands. Now part of Wood Islands (Lighthouse) Provincial Park. The light is open seasonally to the public (for a nominal fee) as a lighthouse and ferry museum operated by a non-profit volunteer community group.

Wood Islands, where the ferry docks.

Directions: Access to the light is just beyond the Visitor Information Centre beside the Northumberland Ferries terminal. Parking is near the lighthouse.

Caution: Steep cliffs outside fence.

Wood Islands Harbour Range

The front range light is a 4.5 m (15 ft.) white tapered "pepper shaker" style situated at the end of the pier leading into the Northumberland Ferries terminal. The rear range light, of the same style, also has a red day marker on the seaward side, but is taller at almost 9 m (30 ft.) on the opposite end of the pier. Both of these lights create a warm welcome to PEI to those arriving from Nova Scotia by ferry. The area provides a picturesque vantage point for viewing the Northumberland ferries entering or leaving the dock.

Wood Islands Front Range.

Directions: Both lights are accessible from a narrow dirt road at Wood Islands (Lighthouse) Provincial Park. Visitors may drive to the edge of the pier and walk out to the lights. There is limited turning space for vehicles.

Caution: Foghorn beside front range; no railings on the pier.

Cape Bear *

This 12-m (40-ft.) white tapered tower sits isolated atop a headland and is surrounded by a dense forest. The light station's position, overlooking the Northumberland Strait, provides a magnificent vista including a glimpse of Nova Scotia on a clear day. This same location, however, has left the tower exposed to the rigors of winter weather blowing in from the Strait resulting in physical damage to the exterior of the light station.

Cape Bear.

Directions: Route 18 makes a ninety-degree turn at Cape Bear. At this point drive east on a dirt road for 200 m (219 yds.) then turn right on a dirt lane and proceed for 100 m (109 yds.) to a short driveway on the right. There is a small parking area beside the lighthouse.

Caution: Steep cliff without fencing.

Murray Harbour Range

The front range hugs the sandy beach at what is known locally as Oldstore Point. (This is a great beach, especially at low tide.) Of traditional tapered design, the tower has a red vertical day marker and is supported by wooden cribbing to prevent erosion. This rather small light has a gray lantern and provides a picturesque backdrop to the surrounding beach and harbour. For sunset lovers, this is an ideal spot to watch the red ball of fire disappear beyond the darkening water, producing a magnificent display of colours. Located 1.4 km (0.9 mi.) from the front range, the rear range is 4 m (13 ft.) higher and may be seen in the distance from the front light. Although situated on private property, a closer view of the rear range is possible from Beach Point wharf.

Directions: On Route 18, east of Murray Harbour village, in the community of Beach Point, turn onto the gravel road marked Beach Road and travel 300 m (328 yds.). (For a beach stroll, park to the side of the road and continue on foot to the left along the sandy beach.) Turn left on a narrow, rough, sandy road for 600 m (656 yds.) to the front range light. (This narrow lane may be flooded with very high tides.) Limited parking and turning space is available beside the light. For a better vantage point to observe the tall tapering rear light, drive along Route 18 towards the village of Murray Harbour and turn right onto Wharf Road. Continue to the wharf, a distance of 400 m (437 yds.), and the light will be visible to the left from the wharf across private land.

Caution: front light—narrow, rough road and foghorn; rear light—private property.

Murray Harbour Front Range.

6 Panmure Head *

Panmure Head light station is located just across the sandy beach causeway on Panmure Island. The 18-m (59-ft.) octagon wooden tower, built in 1853, sits on the extremity of the bluff. The light was automated in 1985. It is now open seasonally to the public for a nominal fee. Visitors can climb the steps and ladders to the lantern five stories up. This high perch provides a panoramic view of Cardigan Bay and the long stretch of sandy beach that parallels the causeway.

Panmure Head.

Directions: Follow Route 347 across Panmure Island causeway and turn right onto the first short dirt road, which leads to a parking and turning area near the light.

7 Georgetown Range

Georgetown Rear Range.

The front range on St. Andrews Point is a small circular metal structure painted with red and white horizontal bands and an open light on the top. The rear range, constructed in the traditional "pepper-shaker" design, may be seen from the road. The tall, slender tower of the rear light makes a strong contrast to the more modern style of the front range. Although more costly to maintain than the newer metal and fiberglass structures, this wooden light invokes a desire to preserve a small part of the maritime heritage of local communities.

Directions: Along Route 17, about 10 km (6 mi.) east of Montague, turn onto a road marked Lower Montague Road and St. Andrews Point. The front light can easily be seen a couple of kilometres along this road. The rear light, on the right, is easily visible from the road across private property.

Caution: Private property.

2. Bays & Dunes

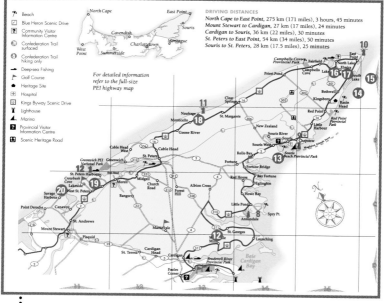

DRIVING DISTANCES

North Cape to East Point, 275 km (171 miles), 3 hours, 45 minutes
Mount Stewart to Cardigan, 27 km (17 miles), 24 minutes
Cardigan to Souris, 36 km (22 miles), 30 minutes
St. Peters to East Point, 54 km (34 miles), 50 minutes
Souris to St. Peters, 28 km (17.5 miles), 25 minutes

For detailed information
refer to the full-size
PEI highway map

● **Adventures**

12 Cardigan Sailing
   Charters

13 Inn at Bay Fortune

14 Red Point Provincial
   Park

15 Basin Head

16 Elmira Railway
   Museum

17 Cycle East

18 Naufrage

19 the Links at
   Crowbush Cove

20 Wild Winds
   Deep-Sea Fishing

🗼 **Lighthouses**

8 Annandale Range

9 Souris East

10 East Point

11 Shipwreck Point
   (Naufrage)

12 St. Peters

Bays and Dunes: Introduction

To find a real sense of what rural life is all about in Prince Edward Island, spend some time in the northeastern end of the province. Free of high-traffic commercial establishments and abundant in nature's splendour, this region exemplifies the appealing notion of "vacation getaway." The southern coastline abounds with inlets and bays, while the north shore is characterized by vast grass-covered sand dunes.

Most of the beaches in this region will not be crowded, even on the warmest summer day. Basin Head, noted for its "singing sands"—caused by an unusual silica texture that results in a squeaking sound when one walks over it—may be busier than others, but even here there is ample room to roam.

Enjoying nature at its best.

Souris, the economic centre of the region, is home to the terminal for the car ferry that travels between Prince Edward Island and the Iles de la Madeleine. Visit the Bays and Dunes region to discover the eastern part of the Confederation Trail—an abandoned railway that is under conversion to a hiking and biking trail to stretch across the entire Island. Also unique to the region is the Bays and Dunes Drive, a route that circles the DayTour area and takes visitors through charming, distinctive communities that offer handcrafted treasures. With so much open space, beautiful vistas await at almost every turn of the highway. However visitors choose to see this region, there is an unmistakable impression that what is important is striking a balance between the land and those who inhabit it.

Cardigan Sailing Charters

Experience the peaceful sensation of a salt-tinged breeze billowing canvas sails, while the boat glides forward, creating a gentle wake as it departs for a relaxing day cruise. There's nothing like salt air to refresh the spirit and awaken the senses.

Capt. John A. Macdonald welcomes a maximum of ten passengers aboard his Island-built 9-m (30-ft.) schooner. Setting sail at 10 A.M. from the docks at Cardigan, the sleek mahogany craft moves out into scenic Cardigan Bay for a five-hour adventure.

Passengers may catch a glimpse of seals or dolphins frolicking near the boat. Inherently curious creatures, they usually investigate vessels passing by. As part of the day's sail, box lunches are provided and heartily devoured, even by the landlubbers aboard, who, by lunchtime, have become sea dogs.

Passengers should pack sunscreen in anticipation of the combination of reflective water and bright sunshine, which may result in rapid sunburn without protection. Those who bring binoculars are always glad they did. Reservations are necessary for Cardigan Sailing Charters.

Adventure

Close to Route 4 at Cardigan
tel. (902)583-2020
Seasonal

Sailing the "Bounding Main."

$$$$

The Inn at Bay Fortune

Bay Fortune
tel. (902)687-3745 or
(860) 296-1348 (in
winter)
Seasonal

Romance, fine dining, and elegant surroundings characterize a stay at the Inn at Bay Fortune. The inn has an unusual structure with two towers behind an early 1900s house with an interesting history of its own. Built by the Broadway playwright Elmer Harris who wrote Johnny Belinda, and later owned as the summer home of actress Colleen Dewhurst, who played Marilla in the Anne of Green Gables movie, the home was purchased and revamped as an inn.

Most of the rooms are located in a low-lying building that forms a three-sided courtyard, provid-

ing outside views and private entrances. Eight of the eleven rooms have working fireplaces, which are ready for guests to light at their leisure. Rooms are comfortable and warmly decorated to create a romantic country atmosphere. The tower room windows overlook

Country living in style.

Fortune Harbour as well as attractive gardens on the property.

Guests will enjoy the renowned upscale dining room with a choice of seating on a glassed-in verandah or inside, where meal presentation is an art in itself. Breakfast is included in the room rates.

Situated a few kilometres from Route 2 in charming Bay Fortune, the inn is close to Souris and makes a lovely, relaxed central location for exploring the eastern end of Prince Edward Island.

$$$$

Red Point Provincial Park

For those who love camping, there are dozens of private and provincial campgrounds scattered across the Island that range from home away from home conveniences to more rustic grounds. Many of the larger private campgrounds, such as Marco Polo Land in Cavendish on the north shore, have a wide array of activities and amenities within the grounds: recreational programs, tennis courts, gift shops, laundromats, camper's stores, dining rooms, heated pools, and, of course, camping sites equipped with flush toilets and hot showers. As many visitors return each year, spaces are often booked well in advance.

On Route 16, 13 km (8 mi.) east of Souris tel.(902) 357-2463 or 652-2356 (in winter) Seasonal

Those in search of a camping experience in a quieter, more natural setting, will find there are many basic campgrounds that offer relaxed, serene surroundings. Red Point Campground is a good example. The 3-ha (7-acre) provincial park has a supervised ocean beach, kitchen shelters, and playgrounds. Recreation and interpretive programs are offered. Several campsites have the convenient flush toilets and hot showers. As with larger private operations, reservations are accepted (after April 1, in this case). Although these smaller parks don't have the range of modern amenities of their more commercial cousins, many campers prefer to escape from modern conveniences and return to nature.

Camping out—a return to nature.

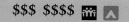

$$$ $$$$

Off Route 16, east
of Souris
tel. (902) 357-2966 or
(902)368-6600 (off-
season)
Seasonal
www.metamedia.pe.
ca/peimuseum

The fisheries museum at Basin Head offers insight into the inshore fishery through displays of gear, boats, and photographs, interpretive exhibits and a newly restored cannery. The wharf, bridge, and fish shacks at Basin Head help create an atmosphere of an inshore fishing village. A lecture series and other events are held here. Call for details.

The museum grounds have a different kind of recreation in store. A popular activity, known as "riding the river," is a refreshing way to cool off on a hot day at Basin Head. A delightful deep-water run that empties into the ocean creates a fast-flowing current that children dive or jump into from the curved footbridge. Some return for the thrill of the leap via the ladders on the side of the wharf, while others are carried to the end of the run about 100 m (330 ft.) away, and walk ashore. Still others begin the adventure on the protected beach inside the run, wading out into the current to be quickly pulled along.

A boardwalk leads to the popular white sandy beach where children play. The beach is supervised in the summer and has a canteen, washrooms, and

Preparing to "ride
the river."

other amenities. The museum maintains a sense of history atop the hill, along with gift shops and food outlets, away from the bustle of the scenic beach area. Admission to the park is free although there is a nominal charge to visit the museum.

"A nice place to relax on beautiful white sand." J.C.

Free

Elmira Railway Museum

Much of Prince Edward Island's colourful railroad past can be relived at the Elmira Railway Station. At its peak, the Prince Edward Island railway had over 400 km (250 mi.) of track and 121 stations. The railway fever that swept the Island created a meandering line that twisted and turned en route to every major (and minor) community and ended at Elmira Station. The crushing railway debt was a deciding factor in the island colony joining Confederation in 1873 on the condition that the Dominion would take over the newest province's railway debt and maintain the rail system.

Route 16A, east of Souris
tel.(902) 357-2481 or (902)368-6600 (in winter)
Seasonal
www.metamedia.pe.ca/peimuseum

Although many of the original buildings of this once bustling terminus have long since been removed, the original station and freight shed remain. A railway car sits on the short section of track still intact beside the station, although it is not open to the public. The station master's office has been restored to convey the organized chaos of a by-gone era.

Down by the station at the end of the line.

Photographs, maps, and artifacts displayed in what were the men's and women's waiting rooms add a visual dimension to understanding the rich heritage created by the Prince Edward Island, Intercolonial and Canadian National Railways.

Visitors can access the Confederation Trail at this museum site and enjoy a hike or bike ride along picturesque wood lots and farmland. (See Cycle East on page 26.)

(See Cycle East on page 26.)

$

Cycle East

Elmira: Route 16A
tel. (902)687-4087
Seasonal

Cyclists travelling along the highway and side roads of Prince Edward Island are a common sight. The gently rolling landscape and stretches of scenic coastline or pasture hold irresistible appeal for many cyclists; even less enthusiastic folk have been inspired to rent a bicycle for a spin in the fresh Island air.

Confederation trail—part of "bike country."

For those who feel reluctant to share a road with four-wheel (or more) vehicles, there is the Confederation Trail. "Mile 0" is at Elmira Railway Museum and continues—in stages—to Tignish, 350 km (217 mi.) away via the abandoned rail line.

Cycle East (one of many bike rental companies throughout the Island) offers CCM mountain bike rentals for the whole family. Bicycles are available at an hourly, daily, or weekly rate at Cycle East in Elmira (or in Souris) with helmets, locks, water bottles, and taxes included in rental fees.

According to owners Cameron Ross and Carol Carter, "Travelling on the Trail is excellent for the novice cyclist because [it] is fairly level with a fine gravel about the consistency of kitty litter. It is also a good [route] for birding and exploring."

$ to $$$ 🏨

Naufrage

For those who love to discover what few others have been able to find, visit Naufrage, a tiny fishing village tucked away behind sand dunes and cliffs. Colourful fishing vessels brighten up the weathered wharves. Cottage rentals make this an ideal spot for a quiet getaway with gorgeous sunsets, sandy beach strolls, and panoramic ocean vistas as the featured entertainment.

On Route 16

Discover true maritime life around the well-protected Naufrage Harbour. There is a narrow deep run that leads to the ocean. A high wooden single-lane bridge crosses the run where the boats return safely to harbour, guided by the lighthouse on a nearby cliff. On warm summer days, children may often be seen jumping and diving off the sides of the run as if it were their own private community swimming pool. This striking little village is an ideal spot for capturing on film the quiet beauty of a community that depends upon the sea for its livelihood.

Discover a secret hideaway at Naufrage.

Beside the run is a lovely little sand beach frequented mainly by locals. It is perfect for sunbathing and beachcombing. It is not unusual to be the only ones to be wiggling your toes in the surf or discovering some washed up treasure from the sea.

Naufrage means "shipwreck," (the first settlers waded ashore after being shipwrecked here in 1760) and the term has been applied to nearby Shipwreck Park, which has a large field with playground equipment and picnic tables. A quaint little bridge and stairs lead into a dense wooded area which has rather undefined but passable pathways. Insect repellent will keep pesky bugs at bay.

Free

Route 350, off Route 2
tel. 1-800-377-8337
Seasonal

The landscape of Prince Edward Island seems ideal for golf courses and there are many fine ones to choose from. Several courses open to the public feature breathtaking ocean views from many of the holes. Scenic courses from nine to eighteen holes, reasonable green fees (ranging roughly between less than twenty dollars to fifty dollars, plus taxes), and varying degrees of difficulty make golfing fun for the entire family. Golf at courses suited to amateurs or tackle the championship-level hazards where the pros play on the Island.

The beautiful clubhouse at Crowbush Cove.

One of the most famous courses is The Links at Crowbush Cove—an 18-hole, par 72—which hosted the Skins Game in 1998. *Golf Digest* designated The Links as the best new Canadian course in 1994, and it was the site of the 1997 Canadian Amateur Golf Championship. The course has a panoramic view of the north shore with nine water holes, and eight holes surrounded by dunes. A computer-controlled irrigation system aims to extend the golfing season into the spring and fall. The modern facilities include guaranteed tee times, pro shop, licensed lounge, refreshments and meals.

"The Links is a beautiful course that makes the game even more fun." E.R.H.

The province operates a number of public courses, such as Mill River Provincial Golf Course (1-800-377-8339), which is ranked as one of the top twenty public courses in Canada, with challenging water hazards and unusual changes in elevation. Brudenell River Provincial Golf Course (1-800-377-8336), like Mill River, is an 18-hole, par 72 (a second course and a golf academy are being added) that has hosted a number of Canadian Professional Golfers' Association (CPGA) events.

$$$$

Wild Winds Deep-Sea Fishing

There are quite a number of deep-sea fishing excursions available around Prince Edward Island. Most of the vessels are based along the northern shore and eastern end of the Island. Some may be chartered for tuna fishing but the majority take groups of people out about 6 km (4 mi.) to fish for cod, mackerel, and herring.

Capt. Charles Pigott operates the Wild Winds, a 13-m (44-ft.) fibreglass fishing boat. Safety approved by the Canadian Coast Guard, the boat has washroom facilities, and all gear and bait are supplied. Trips last about three and one-half hours. Upon returning to Savage Harbour Wharf, the catch will be cleaned, filleted, and bagged for passengers, if desired.

For those whose sea legs are not well broken in, we recommend motion sickness medication before venturing out because the swells may be a little rough—such is the life of fishermen. Captain Pigott doesn't operate in foul weather out of consideration for the safety and comfort of his passengers. In good weather, the refreshing ocean breeze and the thrill of the catch make these trips quite popular.

Savage Harbour
on Route 218
tel. (902)676-2024
Seasonal

Shipping out for a
voyage of adventure.

If visitors drive along the dirt road past the Savage Harbour Wharf area, they will come upon a lovely secluded sand beach that is great for beachcombing.

$$$ 🏨

8 · Annandale Range

At 20 m (66 ft.) the rear range is one of the tallest light structures on Prince Edward Island. A white tower with a red vertical stripe, it is located on the end of Juniper Point. Although the light sits across private property, it is highly visible from the road. The front range is a 5-m (17-ft.) tower situated on a small cliff in a field above the shoreline. The front light is unusual in that it doesn't have the normal lantern on top but rather a pyramid roof capping a tapering tower with the light built into the lower part of the roof area.

Annandale Rear Range.

Directions: To reach the rear range, on Route 310 near Little Pond, follow the road to Annandale Wharf. Turn right onto a paved road at 1 km (0.6 mi.) and continue for a distance of 0.6 km (0.4 mi.). The rear light is straight ahead, across a private field. From the rear light, to see the front range, return 0.6 km (0.4 mi.) to the main road and continue right for 1 km (0.6 mi.) to the wharf. The light is across private property to the left.

Caution: Both lights are on private property.

9 · Souris East *

The Souris East light station helps guide the ferry from the Iles de la Madeleine, among other vessels, into the harbour at Souris. Situated on the end of Knight Point and southeast of the breakwater, the lantern atop the white tapered tower is of the classic round metal design, a rarity on Prince Edward Island. This was the last manned lighthouse on the Island. The area is completely enclosed by a fence, and visitors may view the light only from a short distance.

Souris East.

Directions: From the main highway running through Souris, turn onto MacPhee Avenue (watch for a sign for the Isles de la Madeleine ferry), a distance of 0.8 km (0.5 mi.). Turn left onto Breakwater Street and proceed for about 200 m (220 yds.). The light station is on the right. There is a small driveway and turning space.

Caution: Foghorn; steep cliffs outside fenced area.

East Point*

Situated atop the easternmost extremity of Prince Edward Island, the East Point lighthouse is one of several that are open to the public during the summer months. This wooden octagon light station, built in 1867 and measuring about 19.5 m (65 ft) high, sits in an open field along with the 1908 original fog alarm building. Those who have visited North Cape may exchange their North Cape ribbon in the gift shop for a Traveller's Certificate stating they have toured the island from tip to tip. (Or collect a ribbon here to be turned in at North Cape.)

East Point, twice relocated.

The light was originally built a distance of 0.8 km (0.5 mi.) to the east; however, the wrecking of a British warship in 1882 was blamed on the light's position, and it was moved in 1885 onto the point. In 1908 the wooden tower had to be relocated again slightly further inland of the point due to erosion.

The original fog alarm building is now used as an interpretive centre and craft shop. Tours of the lighthouse (one of the last lights in the province to be automated) are conducted for a nominal fee during the summer months. The light overlooks the meeting of the Gulf of St. Lawrence and Northumberland Strait tides.

Directions: On Route 16 in the community of East Point, follow the signs to the lighthouse. Ample parking and turning space are available near the light.

Caution: Foghorn; extremely steep cliffs.

11 Shipwreck Point (Naufrage) *

This is an unfortunate name for a point of land that is the sight of a light station. Perched in an open field atop a cliff, this white circular tower is 14 m (47 ft.) tall and one of only two concrete towers on Prince Edward Island. Situated across private property, the light can be seen from the road or from the lovely beach on the ocean side of the small bridge in the community's centre.

Directions: Off Route 16, follow the paved road through Naufrage Harbour. The lighthouse is just west of the narrow single-lane bridge that crosses over the entrance to the harbour.

Caution: Private property.

12 St. Peters *

The square tower at St. Peters is 10 m (33.5 ft.) above the water. Accessible by walking down the beach, the light is located on the ocean side of a lagoon. Shifting sand has closed in much of the

original harbour area. This small light, which once safely guided fishing boats into the harbour, now serves only as a warning light along the shoreline. A stroll through what is now an isolated area will reveal parts of the old harbour wharf and the ocean that were once alive with fishermen and their boats. One can only imagine what it was like in days gone by.

St. Peters.

Directions: To view the light: On the east end of Bristol, Route 2, follow a paved road marked St. Peters Harbour for a distance of 1.9 km (1.2 mi.). Continue straight ahead. The pavement ends at 400 m (437 yds.) and continues as a narrow lane for 600 m (656 yds.). The light is visible across the lagoon. Parking and turning is difficult.
To access the light on foot, follow the paved road marked St. Peters Harbour and continue left at 1.9 km (1.2 mi.) to the end of the road (the last section passes several cottages and ends in the sand behind dunes). Walk out to the beach and proceed right to the lighthouse.

Caution: Extremely narrow, rough roads (may be muddy in spring or wet weather).

3. Charlotte's Shore

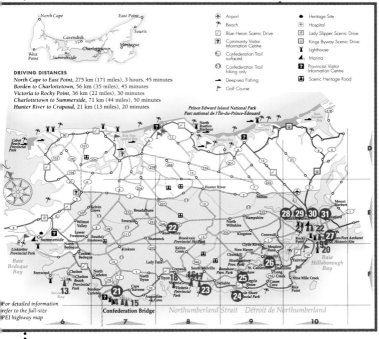

DRIVING DISTANCES
North Cape to East Point, 275 km (171 miles), 3 hours, 45 minutes
Borden to Charlottetown, 56 km (35 miles), 45 minutes
Victoria to Rocky Point, 36 km (22 miles), 30 minutes
Charlottetown to Summerside, 71 km (44 miles), 50 minutes
Hunter River to Crapaud, 21 km (13 miles), 20 minutes

For detailed information refer to the full-size PEI highway map

● Adventures

21 Cavendish Figurines
22 Stanley Pottery
23 Victoria-by-the-Sea
24 Victoria and Argyle Shore Parks
25 Car Life Museum
26 St. Catherines Cove Canoe Rentals
27 Fort Amherst/Port-la-Joye National Historic Site
28 Charlottetown
29 Smooth Cycle
30 Confederation Centre of the Arts
31 The Inns on Great George

‍🕯 Lighthouses

13 Seacow Head
14 Port Borden Pier
15 Port Borden Range
16 Palmer Range (Victoria)
17 Learp's Range
18 Wrights Range
19 Blockhouse Point
20 Warren Cove Range
21 Brighton Beach Range
22 Haszard Point Range

Charlotte's Shore: Introduction

Charlotte's Shore region, locally referred to as the south shore, edges the famous warm waters of the Northumberland Strait. Visitors travelling from New Brunswick, across the Confederation Bridge, will first enter Borden-Carleton, where a Visitor Information Centre at Gateway Village can provide helpful tips about where to go and what to see. A striking patchwork of signature Island colours—red, green, and blue—enlivens farming communities, woodlands, and coastal fishing villages throughout the region. A jaunt inland to the area around Kinkora will lead to the heart of potato-growing country, where fields of potato plants create the illusion of a green sea.

Confederation Bridge.

PEI's famous potatoes, growing row on row.

As the name suggests, Charlottetown is one of the main features of Charlotte's Shore. It is a small capital with a population of less than twenty thousand. But don't be misled by its size. There are luxury accommodations such as the Inns on Great George; historic landmarks such as Province House National Historic Site, where the Fathers of Confederation met in 1864 for the Charlottetown Conference—hence the city's nickname, the birthplace of Confederation; and a rich cultural life with the Confederation Centre of the Arts, featuring live theatre and an increasingly popular musical production called Somewhere in the World.

The abundance of rivers throughout Charlotte's Shore and the normally calm Northumberland Strait make an ideal setting for water-based activities. The beaches are redder compared to the golden sand of the northern coast, but the waves are gentle, the water is warmer, and crowds don't exist. There is no shortage of sites to explore or scenic vistas to enjoy.

Cavendish Figurines

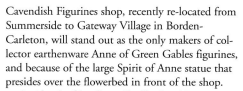

Cavendish Figurines shop, recently re-located from Summerside to Gateway Village in Borden-Carleton, will stand out as the only makers of collector earthenware Anne of Green Gables figurines, and because of the large Spirit of Anne statue that presides over the flowerbed in front of the shop.

Inside, the friendly staff will take visitors on a guided tour of the production facilities where the different stages can be observed, from pouring moulds to the final hand painting. The tour will heighten appreciation of the intricate work that goes into each figurine. After the tour, visitors may browse through the gift shop or bring along their cameras to capture a "live" Anne. The shop has a photo room with different background sets and a collection of vintage clothes that can transform visitors into L. M. Montgomery's classic character, Anne of Green Gables.

"The shop and figurines are highly impressive." P.C.

Adventure

Gateway Village, at the foot of Confederation Bridge in Borden-Carleton tel. (902)437-2663 Open year-round

Jeannette Arsenault displays a Cavendish figurine.

Anne of Green Gables welcomes visitors to Gateway Village.

22 Stanley Pottery

There are several impressive pottery studios around Prince Edward Island that create beautiful pieces for purchase, and where visitors can see potters at work. One example is the studio of Malcolm Stanley, tucked away in the village of Breadalbane, down a narrow little lane off Dixon Road, that leads through dense forest to the studio. The search for the studio is worth the effort. The studio's natural setting is breathtaking and is represented in hand-painted scenes on stoneware and porcelain pottery. Inside, visitors probably will find Malcolm hard at work, throwing a little clay on the wheel.

Malcolm is happy to show how he fashions pieces inspired by his surroundings, including trees and flowers. He often will entertain children with demonstrations while their parents browse through his gallery upstairs. His work includes traditional pieces as well as unique items.

Travel 3 km (2 mi.) along Dixon Road on Route 246, Breadalbane
tel. (902)621-0316
Seasonal; evenings and off-season by chance or appointment

Malcom Stanley "throws a little clay" in his studio.

Free

Victoria-by-the-Sea

There are some Island communities that are queen-like by character or by name. Victoria (also known as Victoria-by-the-Sea) has both the character and the name. Charming little towns are plentiful throughout Prince Edward Island, but Victoria has become one of the most visited communities and popular destinations along Route 10. In fact, more and more people are discovering this unique seaside village, which has become famous for its repertory theatre at the Victoria Playhouse. Here, theatrical productions and musical concerts are held. The

Just off the Trans-Canada Highway
(Route 10)
tel. 1-800-925-2025
(May to September)
or (902)658-2025 for
Victoria Playhouse
Most shops and
cafés open
seasonally

The Victoria Playhouse has become an established repertory theatre.

quiet picturesque streets lined with heritage buildings are perfectly designed for strolling. Parking is provided near the dock where visitors can watch fishing boats unload. At the end of the dock is a restaurant and a number of unique arts and crafts shops in nineteenth-century style buildings. The unique range light is a focal point within the village and there are some lovely cafés within easy walking distance.

On the edge of the town is a provincial park with a warm-water beach, change houses, washroom facilities, and a picnic area. (See Victoria Provincial Park page 38.)

Free

Victoria and Argyle Shore Provincial Parks

Victoria Provincial Park: Just off the Trans-Canada Highway
Argyle Shore: On Route 19
Both parks are seasonal

For those who find pleasure in less crowded beaches visited mainly by locals and not throngs of tourists, the south shore beaches are ideal. There are several provincial beach parks open to the public free of charge. The beaches, often located over a low sandstone embankment, are lined with reddish coloured sand and have shores lapped by gentle waves. The parks usually have washroom and change facilities, although they may not have lifeguards.

One especially beautiful beach, Victoria Provincial Park, is just outside the village of Victoria-by-the-Sea, and a second one is situated a little more to the east, Argyle Shore Provincial Park. At low tide, on either beach, there are usually red sand flats to walk on, warm tidal pools to splash in, and a low surf perfect for swimming.

Undoubtedly, once you have spent an hour or two swimming and playing on the sandy shores, you will be famished. Visitors can spread out a picnic at one of the tables scattered about the grassy area above the beach.

Victoria Provincial Park: a favourite local beach.

Free

Car Life Museum

An unknown source astutely observed that the automobile is "man's greatest invention—until he got into the driver's seat." Journey into the past at the Car Life Museum with the aid of displays that offer insight into the history of the automobile, including various styles of horseless carriages, an 1898 Mason Steamer (yes, some cars truly did run on steam), the Tin Lizzie (Henry Ford's Model T) era, and modern classics. The 1959 pink Cadillac that once belonged to the King of Rock and Roll,

Trans-Canada highway at Bonshaw
tel. (902)675-3555
Seasonal

Elvis Presley, is a favourite among many visitors. For those who loved to watch Don Messer and his Islanders on television, Don's Thunderbird on display here will evoke fond memories. There are over twenty cars exhibited as well as restored tractors and other farm equipment. An area outside features larger-than-life sculpted animals.

A journey into the past.

$

St. Catherines Cove Canoe Rentals Inc.

West off Route 9 on
St. Catherines Road
tel. (902)675-2035
Hourly and daily
rates are per canoe

The West River of Prince Edward Island guarantees a tranquil canoe trip with striking scenery, plenty of bird life (such as bald eagles), and marine life. Placid inland waters through a deep valley make the route perfect for both the novice and seasoned paddler. The tidal river allows paddlers to ride upstream with the incoming water into the Bonshaw Hills and then return a couple of hours later as the tide recedes downstream. (Shorter trips are also available.) Since the tides change daily, it is a good idea to book in advance for the best times.

Paddlers are fitted with Personal Flotation Devices before heading out. Brimmed hats and insect repellent are recommended for the trip. A leisurely paddle allows visitors to fully appreciate the natural beauty that awaits.

Soft adventure on the
West River.

For a small additional fee, paddlers can be taken upriver to Bonshaw so they may do a one-way trip down to owner Andrew Lucock's tiny riverside farm. Andrew enjoys introducing to all visitors his kittens, lambs, goats, calves, rabbits, and hedgehogs.

$$ 🏛 📷

Fort Amherst/Port-la-Joye National Historic Site

Port-la-Joye, the first permanent European settlement on Prince Edward Island, was established by the French in 1720 at this site, near Rocky Point. The settlement, captured by the British in the mid-1700s, was replaced by Fort Amherst. Only the earthworks of the fort remain today.

Off Route 19
tel. (902)672-6350
Seasonal

Visitors may stroll along the grassy grounds that overlook Charlottetown Harbour. Displays, an audio-visual presentation, and bilingual guides highlight the site's history. There is also a period café. Walking trails lead from the Visitor Centre through the woods.

A short drive past the entrance reveals a wide open area where muzzle-loading cannons guard picnic tables scattered near the waterfront. Children enjoy playing on the cannons or investigating the

navigational range lights near the entrance. The picnic tables and the washrooms in the Visitor Centre are wheelchair accessible, but assistance may be necessary to explore the earthworks.

Cannons proudly guard Charlottetown Harbour.

$

Charlottetown, the capital of "the Garden of the Gulf," is where Canada was born, that is, it's the site of the Charlottetown Conference during which federal union—with the exceptions of Prince Edward Island and Newfoundland—was discussed. This small city, which retains its eighteenth-century layout, provides a change of pace from the seaside villages and rolling farmlands found throughout most of the Island. There is much to see and appreciate in this fine historic setting, including neatly kept Victorian houses, lush city parks, and stately places of worship such as the twin Gothic-spire St. Dunstan's Basilica. There is an obvious range of architectural styles as a result of the 1866 fire that swept through the city's commercial core.

Downtown area just off the Trans-Canada Highway
tel. 1-800-955-1864
Some sites are seasonal. Call for details.

Peake's Quay.

Visitors flock to Atlantic Canada's largest art gallery and the museum at Confederation Centre, where the ever-popular Anne of Green Gables musical is performed; the Georgian-style Province House, at the corner of Richmond and Great George Streets, which is where the province's legislature meets; and Victoria Park that has a muzzle-loading gun battery overlooking the harbour.

Where Canada was born.

Perhaps one of the best ways to explore Charlottetown is on foot. A painted blue line along sidewalks leads through some of the city's most interesting areas, including Peake's Quay, the yacht club, monuments, heritage structures and quaint little shops. An array of historic buildings converted into stylish Victorian shops line the picturesque waterfront. Occasionally, performers in period costumes stroll about, setting the historic stage for Canadian Confederation in the city that stakes its claim as Canada's birthplace.

Free ⛹ ♿

Smooth Cycle

There are numerous ways to see and enjoy Charlottetown's small downtown area: on foot; others ride the double-decker bus that visits this area as well as the suburbs; or visitors can rent bicycles by the day or week. For a truly unique perspective of Charlottetown, Smooth Cycle presents Tuesday Tours.

For two hours an experienced guide on wheels takes groups along the scenic waterfront, past historic sites, magnificent churches, and city parks (one of the park stops is for a snack). The commentary, focusing on the city's history, is presented in an interesting and fun fashion.

Before leaving Smooth Cycle's livery at the corner of Prince and Kent Streets, participants are fitted with the proper size bicycle and helmet. Naturally, the ability to ride a bike is the basic requirement, so the tour wouldn't be appropriate for very young children. Although the trip will continue on a rainy day if requested, it probably would be more enjoyable in the sunshine.

Corner of Kent and
Prince Streets,
Charlottetown
tel. (902)566-5530 or
1-800-310-6550
Cycle shop open
year-round
Guided tours
seasonal

Peddling
through the city.

"A great way to see the city." E.R.H.

$$$$

Confederation Centre of the Arts

145 Richmond Street,
Charlottetown
tel. (902)628-1864 or
toll free May through
September 1-800-
565-0278
Open year-round
www.confederationc
entre.com

Most people who come to Charlottetown stay at least long enough to enjoy a performance of what is perhaps Canada's longest running musical, the delightful family classic *Anne of Green Gables*. Each year this mainstage production is accompanied by other performances as part of the Charlottetown Festival at the Confederation Centre of the Arts.

On nice days the Confederation Centre Brass gives a free lunchtime concert. People gather to snack on a hot dog and cool drink while they enjoy the music. For a vibrant, exciting, and lively show of song and dance, catch the original version of

Confederation Centre Brass.

"Somewhere in the World."

"Somewhere in the World" in the outdoor amphitheatre, Monday to Saturday. The show starts at noon and is free, although donations are appreciated. The production features young Canadians of many ethnic origins and celebrates Canada's diverse population. As well as entertaining theatre, there are other forms of culture and heritage at the Confederation Centre: an art gallery, museum, and library, for instance. There are also shops and a restaurant on site.

Free $$$$

The Inns on Great George

There are plenty of inns on Prince Edward Island, from simple country style to five-star luxury accommodations. The Inns on Great George is among the exceptional choices. Situated in the historic district of Charlottetown, the inn is a collection of several landmark buildings, including the original Pavilion and Wellington Hotels. With the two former hotels on either end, the entire block of heritage buildings was carefully restored and renovated to provide a unique yet luxurious atmosphere.

Not only do the inns' attractive exteriors present a lovely streetscape with a range of architectural styles, but the inns offer a variety of accommodations, each with individual character and charm. For example, the Pavilion features twenty-four elegant guest rooms, some with a fireplace, jacuzzi, or claw foot tub, while the Carriage House has spacious one-bedroom units. Families often select the two-floor suites in either the Witter-Coombs House or the Carroll House or, for longer stays, a townhouse flat in the J. H. Down House.

58 Great George Street
tel. (902)892-0606 or
1-800-361-1118
Open year-round
www.innsongreatg
orge.com

Situated just behind Province House, the Inns on Great George are within easy strolling distance from the downtown area and the historic waterfront. Before heading out for a day of sightseeing, guests can enjoy breakfast, included in the varying room rates, served casual-style in the sprawling lobby of the Pavilion.

The "inn" place to stay.

13 **Seacow Head**

This magnificent octagon wooden tower sits 18 m (60 ft.) above water level at the end of a country lane in an open field overlooking the Northumberland Strait. The light was moved further back from its original location on this site to

its present location. From atop the cliff, the eight-sided red lantern projects across to the Confederation Bridge in the distance, making a picturesque scene.

Directions: Follow signs for Fernwood on Route 119 to a T intersection. Turn left on the dirt road for Seacow Head. The light is clearly visible from this point. Turn right on the first dirt lane. There is parking and space to turn around at the light.

Seacow Head.

Caution: Steep cliffs; discarded barbed wire hidden in the grass near the light station.

14 **Port Borden Pier**

On the outer end of the old ferry pier, this tapered wooden tower is 8.5 m (28 ft.) in height. Once a welcome sight as the ferry arrived from New Brunswick, the tower demonstrates how changes make some lights obsolete. With the building of the Confederation Bridge and discontinuation of the New Brunswick ferry system, very few vessels now enter the harbour. The lonely light sits at one end of the former ferry dock, waiting for its lantern to be extinguished forever.

Directions: The light can be seen from the barricades leading to the former ferry docks or from the parking lot of Heron Woodworking on Carleton Street in Borden-Carleton.

Port Borden Range (Decommissioned Lights)

15

The rear range sits beside the parking lot of Heron Woodworking and is a 13-m (41-ft.) square tapered tower with a red vertical day marker. The front range, also with a red day marker, is 152.5 m (500 ft.) across an open field near the water. These two lights easily demonstrate how the range light system works as both range towers are clearly visible from the side. As a vessel enters the harbour it lines up the light projecting from the higher rear range light directly above the light of the lower front range. As long as the two lights are one above the other, the vessel is safely in the channel. The range light system is now being replaced with a single sector light (a white light that turns red or green when a vessel is off course) as well as satellite navigational systems.

Directions: View the range from the barricades leading to the former ferry docks or from the parking lot of Heron Woodworking on Carleton Street just east of the Gateway Village in Borden-Carleton.

Port Borden Rear Range.

Palmer Range (Victoria)*

16

While the front range is simply a skeleton tower on the shoreline, the rear range is most unusual: the latter is actually Palmer rear range as well as Learp's front range. This is made possible with two different lights erected to point in two separate directions in the lantern. Reportedly the second oldest light structure on Prince Edward Island, Palmer rear range is an 11-m (35-ft.) white tapered tower with a red vertical day marker. Located beside the waterfront parking area, it has also been used as the Victoria Seaport Museum with displays of photos depicting the seafaring heritage of the community.

Directions: In Victoria, travel to the west end of the bridge at the head of Victoria Harbour on Water Street.

Palmer Rear Range/ Learp's Front Range.

17 Learp's Range

As indicated for Palmer range, the Palmer rear range is also the Learp's front range. Learp's rear range is located 852 m (2,795 ft.) back into the community across private lands and is a similar tower to the front light. Viewed from the roadway, this tall tapering white structure's picturesque setting admits flowering gardens against a backdrop of rolling farmland all covered by a deep blue sky. While some range lights require a bit of effort to locate, the front and rear ranges in Victoria are highly visible.

Learp's Rear Range.

Directions: To see Learp's front range, in Victoria travel to the west end of the bridge at the head of Victoria Harbour. To see the "Rear" range, follow the Blue Heron Scenic Drive (Route 10) west through Victoria. The light is located across private property to the right.

18 Wrights Range

The front range is visible from a distance on the south side of Paul's Bluff. This 4-m (12-ft.) white square tower is located across private property. Situated at the end of a wide expanse of farmland, the sight of this tiny tower, with Victoria in the distance, creates the essence of PEI—fishing, farming and a quiet rural lifestyle. The rear range is 10 m (32 ft.) and is situated on the lawn of a farm. This neatly maintained tower, with a bright Canadian flag fluttering in the wind, is a perfect observation point to enjoy the vistas created by lush foliage edging a tranquil blue sea. Although the light is beside the road, permission should be obtained from the owner of the property before crossing.

Wrights Rear Range.

Directions: Drive west on the Blue Heron Scenic Drive (Route 10) through Victoria. Turn left on Route 116W (Tryon) to see the front light to the left. Continue straight ahead to Beach Light Road, a distance of 1.2 km (0.7 mi.). Turn left on this road and proceed to the end, a distance of 700 m (765 yds.).

Caution: Private property; limited parking and turning.

Blockhouse Point *

Also known as the Rocky Point lighthouse, this is a beautiful lighthouse tower attached to the corner of a two-storey dwelling that overlooks the entrance to Charlottetown Harbour. Blockhouse Point is the only light structure of this design on PEI. While many of the keeper's dwellings were either small attachments to the light tower or a separate building, this lovely house with its picket fence, red window trim and neatly maintained lawns is picture-perfect. Wonderful vistas of Charlottetown Harbour are possible from atop the cliff near the light station. During the summer the keeper's house is occupied—please respect their privacy.

Blockhouse Point.

Directions: Off Route 19, continue straight ahead on the road past the entrance to Fort Amherst/Port-la-Joye National Historic Site (the pavement changes to dirt road at this point) for 1 km (0.6 mi.). Parking and turning space are available.

Warren Cove Range

The front and rear range lights are accessible on the grounds of Fort Amherst/Port-la-Joye National Historic Site. Both are standard white tapered towers and an easy walk for visitors to the site. Children especially enjoy these range lights as they may safely approach them over mowed grass walkways.

Warren Cove Rear Range.

Directions: Off Route 19, enter the driveway leading to Fort Amherst/Port-la-Joye National Historic Site. The rear range will be visible across a field to the left; the front range will be about 330 m (1,080 ft.) beyond, nearer the shoreline.

21

Brighton Beach Range

Brighton Beach Rear
Range (top) and
Front Range (bottom).

The tapered front white tower is situated on cribbing that projects into the Charlottetown Harbour near Victoria Park along Charlottetown's waterfront. Although this tower is of standard design, its position along the shoreline near beautiful homes is impressive. The light is highly visible from the Park Roadway (Victoria Park) or may be examined close-up. Resembling a thread spool, the rear Y-shaped concrete tower is located between private homes on Queen Elizabeth Way. Although extremely modern in design, and not considered a lighthouse by traditional standards, the tower is unique in that there isn't another similar light structure on PEI. It is easily visible from the street.

Directions: The front light is visible from Park Roadway that runs parallel to the shoreline in Victoria Park and is accessible from York Lane. The rear light is visible about 400 m (1,300 ft.) beyond the front light on Queen Elizabeth Way.

22

Haszard Point Range

The front range tower is situated on the east side of the entrance to Charlottetown Harbour. Located 651m (711 yds) from the front range is the rear tower. Although these range lights are somewhat unusual for PEI, having a black day marker as opposed to the usual red one, they are not shown on the highway map as they aren't readily accessible. They may, however, be viewed from a distance and would be of interest to lighthouse-lovers in search of different types and styles of structures.

Directions: Route 1A between Kinlock and Tea Hill leads to the front range. The light can be seen on the water side of the highway at the end of an unidentified lane. As this lane is not a public roadway, access to the light is restricted. Route 1A between Cross Roads and Tea Hill leads to the rear range. Follow a paved road on south side of the highway. The rear range light is across a private field at the end of this road. As with the front range, the rear range tower can only be observed from a distance.

Caution: Private lane not for public use; private property.

4. Anne's Land

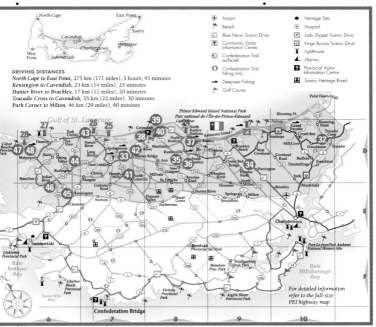

DRIVING DISTANCES
North Cape to East Point, 275 km (171 miles), 3 hours, 45 minutes
Kensington to Cavendish, 23 km (14 miles), 25 minutes
Hunter River to Brackley, 17 km (11 miles), 20 minutes
Tracadie Cross to Cavendish, 35 km (22 miles), 30 minutes
Park Corner to Milton, 46 km (29 miles), 40 minutes

Map legend:
- ✈ Airport
- 🕊 Beach
- ☑ Blue Heron Scenic Drive
- ❓ Community Visitor Information Centre
- ◐ Confederation Trail surfaced
- ◑ Confederation Trail hiking only
- ⚓ Deep-sea Fishing
- 🏴 Golf Course
- ♠ Heritage Site
- ✚ Hospital
- ☑ Lady Slipper Scenic Drive
- ☑ Kings Byway Scenic Drive
- ⚑ Lighthouse
- ⚓ Marina
- ❓ Provincial Visitor Information Centre
- 🏛 Scenic Heritage Road

For detailed information refer to the full-size PEI highway map

● Adventures

32 Outdoor Pursuits

33 Mr. Snorkel Adventures

34 Cheeselady's Gouda

35 New Glasgow Lobster Suppers

36 Prince Edward Island Preserve Company

37 North Rustico Harbour

38 Rainbow Valley Family Fun Park

39 Prince Edward Island National Park

40 Green Gables

41 Geppetto's Workshop

42 Prince Edward Island Marine Aquarium

43 Anne of Green Gables Museum

44 Woodleigh Replicas and Gardens

45 Kensington Train Station and Market

46 Indian River Music Festival

47 Emily of New Moon Television Set

48 Malpeque Cove and Sundance Cottages

⚑ Lighthouses

23 Covehead Harbour

24 North Rustico Harbour

25 New London Range

26 Cape Tryon

27 Malpeque Outer Range

28 Cabot Beach Provincial Park

Anne's Land: Introduction

The central north shore region of Prince Edward Island is peppered with sites related to the renowned fictional heroine Anne of Green Gables, made famous by author Lucy Maud Montgomery. The character of Anne may seem to predominate the region, especially for visitors who come to see the areas that inspired Montgomery's writing.

A land stretching to the sea.

However, part of her inspiration arose from the pastoral beauty of the region, another dimension that draws many visitors. For instance, the Prince Edward Island National Park, overlooking the Gulf of St. Lawrence, is one of Canada's smallest parks at 31 sq. km (12 sq. mi.), but it ranks only after Banff and Jasper as the most popular. Consisting of freshwater ponds, saltwater marshes, woodlands, and beautiful sandy beaches, the park offers natural attractions, including walking trails and abundant bird life, along with campgrounds and swimming. Other popular spots within the park are Green Gables and the exquisite Dalvay-by-the-Sea Inn.

The landscape that inspired Lucy Maud Montgomery.

There is undoubtedly a wide range of commercial attractions in Anne's Land, especially around Cavendish with such sites as Rainbow Valley. Many of these are geared to families, or the young at heart, and children in particular seem to enjoy the seemingly endless availability of activities.

For those who seek a slower pace, there are ample opportunities to circumvent the busier tourist spots in Anne's Land. Coastal scenes of sprawling sand dunes and jagged sandstone cliffs seem to glow in the light of a rising or setting sun. Smaller communities offer quaint tea stops and fine crafts and harbour historic treasures such as St. Augustine's—the Island's oldest Catholic church— in South Rustico. Visit the Rustico region, home to many Acadian families. Whatever pace visitors wish to keep, Anne's Land has something for everyone.

Outdoor Pursuits

Paddling in a 7-m (24-ft.) open-water canoe is an exciting adventure. Patterned after the traditional canoe originally used by local Mi'kmaq, this sturdy craft will accommodate up to seven paddlers plus a qualified guide. Previous paddling experience is not necessary as John Hughes, a former physical education teacher, gives instruction prior to departure.

A trip on the expansive Tracadie Bay may include plying the inland waters behind massive sand dunes that shelter the bay from the Gulf of St. Lawrence. Stops are made along the Blooming Point sandspit. The paddling journey features expert interpretive information on the region and a magnificent view of the shoreline, bay, and seabirds.

John offers a variety of other outings, including fall paddles to a secluded cabin along Winter River.

Tracadie Harbour
Wharf
tel. (902)672-2000
Seasonal
http://members.xoom.
com/outdr_prsts

More than a canoe trip in Tracadie Bay.

$$$

Daily departures to
New London Bay
from Stanley Bridge
on Route 6
tel. (902)894-7552
Seasonal

Snorkelling is usually associated with the turquoise
waters of southern climes, watching an array of
colourful tropical fish. But snorkelling off parts of
Prince Edward Island can be equally fun. True, the
temperature of the ocean is a little different (about
21ºC or 70ºF), but a wetsuit comes in handy. The
underwater life features a collection of lobster, crab,
flatfish, large snails, clam and mussel beds.

Undersea adventure
along the north shore
awaits the curious.

Mr. Snorkel Adventures operates a number of
snorkelling tours along the National Park shoreline.
Participants are transported by Zodiac to a quiet,
shallow bay or cove where leisurely floating allows a
clear view to the bottom while breathing through a
snorkel. Visitors are provided with wetsuits and
other gear, including weight belts for those who
wish to dive for a closer look.

Children under eight years of age are not per-
mitted to snorkel on the four-hour trip. Half-day
rentals or guided tours with lunch are also available.

$$$$ 🏛

Cheeselady's Gouda

Martina Terbeek, known as the Cheeselady, comes from a long line of Dutch cheese-makers. On her Island family farm, they use the milk from their own Holsteins to make cheese using traditional Dutch recipes with unique flavours. Martina has opened her production facilities to the public so they can see how the cheese is made and sample the tasty varieties. A short video in French or English summarizes the lengthy process of cheese-making. The overweight sizes of gouda come in eight flavours, including herb, peppercorn, and garlic, as well as mild (aged less than four months), medium (aged four to ten months), aged (up to a year), and extra old (aged more than a year).

The family farm animals are usually available for a visit: cows, calves, sheep, lambs and even llamas welcome a few moments in the spotlight. The farm cats and dog may also stop by for a little attention from visitors.

Winsloe North, Route 223, 8 km (5 mi.) off Route 2 tel. (902)368-1506 Open year-round except Sundays

Say "Cheese, please."

A touch of Holland.

Free

New Glasgow Lobster Suppers

Route 258 at
New Glasgow
tel. (902)964-2870
Seasonal

Lobster suppers are
a tradition in PEI.

Lobster is king.

A visit to Prince Edward Island wouldn't be complete without partaking in a traditional lobster supper. As the lobster season varies from one area to another on the Island, there is usually an abundant supply.

New Glasgow Lobster Suppers, one of many fine options, is an original, serving delicious meals since 1958. Not far from Cavendish Beach, the fully licensed restaurant overlooks the lovely River Clyde. The menu includes baked goods from their own kitchen, starting with fresh rolls. There is a delicious selection of seafood chowder, homemade

soup, steamed mussels, fresh garden salad, potato salad, and coleslaw. Leave room for the main course: a fresh-from-the-pound lobster served in the shell with melted butter for dipping. Alternatives to lobster include roast beef, sweet ham, or breaded scallops. For dessert there is a wide selection of pies, ice cream, or (in season) strawberry shortcake. A children's menu is available.

Don't miss out on a traditional Island feast, fresh from the sea.

"Scrumptious, abundant food in a welcoming atmosphere." P.C.

$$$$

Prince Edward Island Preserve Company

Unique homemade preserves are the specialty at Bruce MacNaughton's Prince Edward Island Preserve Company. Savour surprising combinations made from fresh local fruit, such as raspberry and champagne, or lemon and ginger marmalade with Amaretto. Visitors are welcome to sample the delectable preserves.

Located in New Glasgow along a meandering river in a renovated 1913 butter factory, the Preserve Company has windows in one wall of the gift and craft shop through which visitors can glimpse the process of preserve-making on site. The name of the product being prepared and bottled is displayed.

Individual bottles and a variety of gift packages with a range of gourmet foods are available in the gift shop. Few people leave empty-handed! Visitors can also enjoy a delicious meal at Café on the Clyde, the lovely restaurant on site, serving meals from breakfast to dinner. Evening reservations are recommended. Call (902)964-4305. The Preserve Company also operates an active year-round mail order service throughout Canada and the United States.

On Route 224 in New Glasgow
tel. (902)964-2524 or 1-800-565-5267
Seasonal
www.preservecompany.com

Preserving a little of the Island, in New Glasgow.

Free

Off Route 6 at
North Rustico

There are dozens of quaint coastal villages scattered throughout Prince Edward Island, and among the prettiest is North Rustico Harbour. The community is situated just outside the national park and is part of the Rustico region where the Acadian heritage lingers audibly in the accent of residents. North Rustico Harbour is picture perfect: colourful fishing boats tied to the wharf, weathered fishing shacks, and panoramic vistas of the Gulf of St. Lawrence. The community has created a charming harbourside boardwalk clinging to the edge of the roadway leading into the village. With ample parking and wheelchair accessibility, the walkway provides a pleasant stroll beside the tranquil water, as well as a perfect vantage point for viewing the village of North Rustico.

A picture-perfect
fishing village.

Many visitors browse in local craft shops and take photos of the unique little lighthouse that is attached to a keeper's dwelling. (See North Rustico lighthouse page 70.) Edging the village on the west is North Rustico Beach (with parking and change facilities), part of the Prince Edward Island National Park .

Free

Rainbow Valley Family Fun Park

Original and well-run commercial attractions are densely clustered in the popular Cavendish area. One that is great fun for everyone is Rainbow Valley, which began as a family operation several decades ago. The 16-ha (40-acre) park has continually expanded by adding new adventures while maintaining the idea of a clean, well-maintained, fun place to visit. Visitors can spend hours enjoying water rides of all kinds: sea bikes, paddleboats, rowboats, motorized boats, a tour boat, water slides, a flume ride, as well as a mono rail, roller coaster, and the Dark Ride (the rum-running days recreated). There are live animals to pet and live animated performances. There are plenty of activities for all ages, from tiny tots to adults. The park also has food services or visitors may bring a picnic lunch.

Many people who visited Rainbow Valley as children return with their own children—the best kind of recommendation.

Route 6 in Cavendish
tel. (902)963-2221
Seasonal

Adventure under the rainbow, in Cavendish.

"A fun family spot." G.R.H.

"A beautiful, imaginative theme park run by a family that dares to be creative." P.C.

$$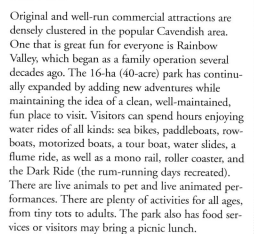

Prince Edward Island
National Park

Entrances off
Routes 6, 13 and 15
between Cavendish
and Tracadie
tel. (902)672-6350
Open year-round;
some facilities are
seasonal.

A stretch of 40 km (25 mi.) along the north shore, covering a surprising range of terrain within a small area, has been preserved as the Prince Edward Island National Park. The park is highlighted by massive grass-covered sand dunes and supervised, serviced beaches, with some of the warmest water to be found in Atlantic Canada. Also protected within the park are salt marshes (perfect for bird-watching), tidal pools, sandstone cliffs, and pockets of forest that shelter a local variety of wildlife. In addition to beach swimming, the park also provides facilities for camping, hiking, cycling and sports such as golf and tennis. A good hard-surfaced

The beach life lasts
all summer in
Cavendish.

road, the Gulf Shore Parkway, runs parallel to the beach behind the sand dunes throughout most of the park—being flat with a refreshing Gulf breeze and coastal views, it is perfect for biking. Summer activities also include bird-watching, beach walks, and campfires. Visitors to the park flock to Green Gables, the inspiration for L. M. Montgomery's fictional home of Anne, and the elegant Dalvay-by-the-Sea Inn at the east end of the park. Information centres have been established at the park entrances near Cavendish and Brackley to supply details about facilities and activities offered. Dwell in the lap of luxury or camp beneath the stars; either way, the Prince Edward Island National Park is a striking and hospitable area to vacation for days at a time, or just visit for a day.

$ 🏛   ♿   ⛰   📷

Green Gables

Most people go to Green Gables to see the mid-1800s house and farm that was the fictional setting for L. M. Montgomery's classic novel, *Anne of Green Gables*. The house and grounds, originally owned by relatives of the author, now recreate memorable scenes from Anne of Green Gables—fact and fiction seem to become one in this charming Victorian setting. In Anne's room are artifacts from the story, including a slate like the one Anne cracked over Gilbert Blythe's head.

An interesting aspect of the Green Gables property is the walking trails. Both of the trails—the Haunted Woods (1.6 km or 1 mi.) and Balsam Hollow (1 km or 0.6 mi.) Trails—appear in the *Anne* story. Visitors familiar with Montgomery's novels will surely hear echoes of Anne's voice along the familiar trails. For those not acquainted with the novels, a pleasant woodland stroll past gentle streams awaits. (Grades are fairly gentle, although in places there are some steps to climb.) Tasteful signs explain aspects of the trails, including the famous Lover's Lane.

Off Route 6 in
Cavendish
tel. (902)672-6350
Seasonal; off-season
visits by request.

Following in Anne's
footsteps.

One of the best times to really enjoy the peace and tranquillity on these trails is to arrive early in the morning. Once the house opens to the public at 9 A.M. the number of people walking the trails increases.

There is an admission fee to the house and barn (save the visit for a rainy day).

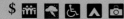

Geppetto's Workshop

Founds Mills on
Route 238, off Route
6
tel. (902)886-2339
Seasonal; closed
Sundays
Off-season by
appointment

David Powell, co-owner of Geppetto's Workshop, even looks the part of the silver-haired marionette-maker from the famous tale of *Pinocchio*. David and his wife, Doris, welcome visitors to the unique shop they have established in their Founds Mills home. This energetic retired couple delight in sharing their imaginative creations with those young at heart. Visitors are treated to a demonstration of how marionettes "come to life."

Pinocchio is the most popular among their array of puppets, marionettes and toys, perhaps due to the unique "growing nose" or the magical way that "Geppetto" makes Pinocchio come alive. Children and adults are captivated by the non-electronic characters and toys.

Doris and David
Powell, being young
at heart.

Both former teachers, the Powells moved to the area to retire, but the popularity of their business has allowed for only semi-retirement. When the shop is closed, they are busy developing new ideas or filling mail orders from around the world.

"Clever ideas, skillfully crafted to enrich everyone's imagination." P.C.

Free

Prince Edward Island Marine Aquarium

Established many years ago along the New London Bay shoreline, the Marine Aquarium has more than marine life in store. Of course, the main display area features a large number of viewing tanks with marine life and fish native to the Island. There is also Manor of Birds in another display hall that is billed as North America's finest private collection of mounted birds (there are over seven hundred). A smaller area off the same hall has a collection of Maritime fur-bearing animals. Yet another section houses Canada's largest display of butterflies collected from around the world.

Just off Route 6 at Stanley Bridge
Seasonal

Outside, there is a small seal pool where children can watch several of these playful creatures up close. An attendant often allows youngsters to help feed the seals, which seems to be a big draw.

There are also interpretive displays depicting the life cycle of the oyster and harvesting Irish Moss, an Island crop that involves raking in the valuable sea product for commercial use in the chemical and food industries.

Feeding time for the seals.

Anne of Green Gables Museum

Park Corner on
Route 20
tel. (902)436-7329 or
1-800-665-2663
Seasonal

Visitors to this museum can relive the scene in *Anne of Green Gables* in which Matthew picks up Anne for the first time in his horse-drawn carriage. The ten-minute ride meanders through the fields and gardens of the museum property. An hour-long excursion to a private beach is also available, perhaps before taking tea in the Shining Waters Tea Room on site.

Originally the home of Montgomery's aunt and uncle, John and Annie Campbell, Lucy Maud spent summers here as a youngster and was married in the parlour. Today, George Campbell continues

Reliving the days of the horse and carriage.

many of the family traditions, including having tea and helping guests try their hand at planting seed potatoes.

The homestead and Shining Waters Tea Room and Craft Shop are open seasonally to the public.

"The Campbell family goes out of their way to make each visit memorable; whether planting your own potatoes or being married in the same room as L. M. Montgomery. Notably hospitable." P. C.

Woodleigh Replicas and Gardens

Centred on 18 ha (45 acres) of lush lawns and colourful English gardens, stands a 9-m (30-ft.) reproduction of Admiral Nelson's column surrounded by over thirty miniature scale replicas of the most famous castles and cathedrals from the British Isles. Smaller structures include Yorkminster, Anne Hathaway's cottage, and the Temple of Flora. There are some replicas that visitors can walk through, such as the two-stories-high Dunvegan Castle, complete with dungeon. After nine years of construction, the massive Tower of London is an impressive sight. Reproductions of the Crown Jewels grace the White Tower, while an underground tunnel leads to the Bloody Tower, providing an excellent adventure for children who love to explore.

Simply strolling around the English gardens is delightful. Children love to run through the maze or climb the Look-out Tower perched on a hilltop. Smaller children will be entertained in the play area not far from the Water Gardens.

Begun as a private project by Ernest Johnstone following World War II, Woodleigh Replicas has grown from several small pieces to a major attraction. In addition to brick walkways, a new food service and gift shop are part of an upgrading program for the property.

Near Route 101 in Burlington
tel. (902)836-3401
Seasonal

Meeting in the castle.

$$

Kensington Train Station and Market

On Route 20, near
the intersection of
Routes 2 and 6
tel. (902)836-3031
Seasonal

Kensington, a former railway centre, is home to a restored train station, one of the few stone stations on the Island. To help preserve and commemorate the rich railway heritage that the original Prince Edward Island railway developed during its years of operation, a museum has been established at the station. It includes a diesel engine and caboose.

Every Saturday morning during the summer the station is bustling with a Farmer's Market. Using the former freight shed as well as parts of the station platform, vendors display their wares. Freshly cut flowers, succulent fruits and vegetables, and lovingly created crafts are all available. Enterprising children set up miniature stands to feature handmade jewelry.

Saturday market at Kensington Station.

After selecting some prized crafts or a bag of freshly picked fruit, find out a little more about the area at the Visitor Information Centre inside the station. There are plenty of brochures and the staff have good suggestions for things to see and do throughout the region.

Free

Indian River Festival of Music

St. Mary's Church in Indian River, on the shores of Malpeque Bay, is home to the Indian River Festival of Music each summer. The Festival features national and internationally renowned choirs, chamber groups, and musicians performing music of the early, baroque, classical, and modern periods. During June and July there is a concert series of performances, usually on Sunday evenings, and the Festival culminates in five-seven days of performances in late July, early August. As well as fine music, the festival offers various related educational and interactive experiences: workshops, master's classes, pre-concert talks, and during the first week of August, activities and music at a Medieval Faire held outside on the grounds of the church.

On Route 104 at Indian River, just off Route 20 near Kensington.
June, July & August
tel. (902) 836-4933
ind.fest/pei.sympatic
o.ca
www3.pei.sympatico.
ca./ind.fest/INDEX.
HTM

St. Mary's Church is gaining an international reputation among world-class musicians because of the pure acoustics of its all-wood gothic interior. Built in 1902 and designed by William Critchlow Harris, the church's native woods enhance instrumentals and vocals, and provide some of the finest acoustic sounds in the world.

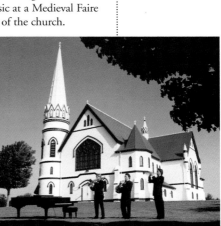

The 1999 schedule includes the Nova Scotia Mass Choir, June 6; the Arthur Leblanc Quartet, July 4, and instrumentalists Mela Tenenbaum and Yosif Feigelson, August 7. Contact the Festival for complete schedule of events and times.

St. Mary's Church has a reputation for providing pure acoustic sound.

$$$

Emily of New Moon Television Set

Off Route 20 at
Malpeque
tel. (902)836-8945
Seasonal

The main house in the television series.

The new Canadian television series *Emily of New Moon*, based on L. M. Montgomery's fictional character Emily, is filmed on location at Cabot Beach Provincial Park overlooking Malpeque Bay. When the crews are not filming, visitors can stroll through the woods and catch a behind-the-scenes glimpse of the period television setting.

Situated in a small booth at the park's picnic area, costumed guides will describe the many scenes and sights associated with the TV series. Highlights include a small lighthouse that was flown to the site, the exterior of an almost hidden house in the sand dunes, a graveyard (built in the woods when needed), a general store, and the main house in the program. An authentic schoolhouse on the property is also used for filming.

The Disappointed House, where Emily and her friends play, overlooks the main beach at Cabot Park.

Children, especially, enjoy discovering how a TV production creates illusions with exteriors of buildings and props.

Cabot Beach Provincial Park is the largest day-use park in western Prince Edward Island. It offers a supervised ocean beach, an activity centre, playground, and interpretive programs such as nature walks with staff naturalists.

Free $

Malpeque Cove and Sundance Cottages

There are charming cottages throughout Prince Edward Island—some for rent, others privately owned—but the region near Cavendish is truly "cottage country," where various levels of accommodations are available for a wide range of prices. Both nightly and weekly cottage rentals are available; however, their popularity during high season means advance booking is best. Lowering vacation costs by preparing your own meals while gaining more spacious accommodations, are great advantages to cottage rental. The following are just two fine examples of the many options on the Island.

Sundance Cottages: Twelve beautifully appointed upscale cottages have decks with an ocean view in Cavendish. With everything provided in the cottages for a true vacation, including a microwave, dishwasher, barbecue, and picnic table, the property includes a heated pool, gym, laundromat, complimentary mountain bikes, and a garden from which guests may select fresh veggies for dinner. Deluxe units feature a four-person jacuzzi and two baths. Comfort and ease are at your fingertips, leaving lots of leisure time to explore the Island or just kick back at the beach with a good book.

Sundance Cottages: On Route 6, east of Cavendish intersection on MacCoubrey Lane tel. (902)963-2149 or 1-800-565-2149 www.peisland.com/sundance/cottages.htm

Malpeque Cove Cottages: On Route 105, near Cabot Beach Provincial Park tel. (902)836-5667 or 1-888-283-1927 www.cycor.ca/kcap/pages/bryanton/index.htm

"These cottages are immaculate, modern, and relaxing." P.C.

Malpeque Cove Cottages

Malpeque Cove Cottages: Watching the sun set from the covered deck of one of these fully equipped housekeeping cottages is the pinnacle of serenity. Situated on 1 ha (3 acres) overlooking the scenic fishing harbour at Malpeque, these two- and three-bedroom units are modern and spacious. It is about a five-minute walk from these cottages to Cabot Beach Provincial Park.

"Spotless, roomy, and comfortable with a picturesque view." P. C.

$$$$ 🏨

Lighthouses

Covehead Harbour *

Used as the base for the national park's interpretive programs, this 8-m (27-ft.) pepper-shaker style light is situated in the dunes overlooking the beach at Stanhope Cape in Prince Edward Island National Park. (During the daytime in the summer, a fee is charged to enter the park.) A plaque attached to the

lighthouse gives details on the Yankee Gale, the wicked storm of 1851 in which many American seamen died. The Old Stanhope Cemetery, located within the national park, contains graves of the drowned seafarers.

Covehead Harbour.

Directions: Beside the Gulf Shore Parkway, the paved road that runs parallel to the ocean through Prince Edward Island National Park, near Stanhope.

Caution: Foghorn; roadside parking.

North Rustico Harbour *

The lighthouse at North Rustico Harbour is perhaps one of the most picturesque on the Island. This tapered tower, with the addition of a small house to the rear, now sits amongst a number of fishing sheds and homes. The light has been moved several times due to the eroding shoreline, which

North Rustico Harbour.

had threatened to dislodge the light station. Perched on a slight rise of land, it overlooks the ocean from the centre of the village, located a few kilometres from North Rustico on Route 6 (see North Rustico Harbour in the Adventures section, page 58). Although it is possible to walk around the lighthouse, please respect the adjoining private property.

Directions: Leave Route 6 at North Rustico and continue towards North Rustico Harbour. Parking is available at the end of the road near the lighthouse.

Caution: Adjoining private property.

New London Range *

The front range light is a skeleton tower on the beach. The rear range is a traditional style light tower with attached house located about 300 m (1,000 ft.) inland from the front light. The rear range has a red vertical day marker on the seaward face. Both lights are operated seasonally. The tapered sides of this structure is fairly unique in that there are only a couple of lights of this style left in operation, and it is the only one of this design on PEI to be used as a range light.

Directions: To reach the rear range light, leave Route 20 at French River on the paved Cape Road (beside the Irving station). At 1.5 km (0.9 mi.) turn right at the intersection onto a gravel road and proceed 1.6 km (1 mi.) to the end. The light will be on the right along a private driveway. The former keeper's house is leased, so please respect the privacy of the occupants. The front range skeleton may be reached by following the trail leading toward the beach.

New London Rear Range.

Cape Tryon *

This 12-m (39-ft.) white square tower is situated in a perfect place for a picnic. Perched on the extremity of Cape Tryon beyond lush potato fields, it is operated year-round. The original one-and-one-half-storey house with tower was relocated due to eroding banks. The present tower was constructed in 1905 and automated in 1962. Although the light is well photographed, the dirt road that leads to it is a little difficult to find.

Directions: Leave Route 20 at French River on the paved Cape Road (beside the Irving station). At 1.5 km (0.9 mi.) turn left at the intersection onto a gravel road. At 0.9 km (0.6 mi.) turn right onto a very narrow dirt road. Follow this single lane for 1 km (0.6 mi.) to the light. There is ample space to turn around at the light.

Caution: Steep cliffs beyond fence; narrow single-lane dirt road. The field beyond the fence, on the land side of the light, is private property.

Cape Tryon.

Malpeque Outer Range

The front range light, a 6-m (20-ft.) tapered tower, is located near the shoreline and should be observed from the beach as it is across private property. The rear range of the same height is situated in a field beside a private lane but is visible from the public road. Although it can not be approached by

foot, it is uniquely Prince Edward Island to find a range light sitting in the middle of a field beyond the view of the ocean. This visual combination, representing agriculture and the sea, is characteristic of the Island's heritage.

Directions: On Route 20 at Darnley, drive 2.9 km (1.8 mi.) on the paved Profitts Point Road (the pavement ends at 2.7 km

Malpeque Rear Range.

or 1.7 mi.). The rear range will be on the right, across private property. To reach the beach near the front range, drive back towards Route 20 a distance of 0.8 km (0.5 mi.) and turn left onto a dirt road. Park beside the sand dunes after driving approximately 1 km (0.6 mi.) and walk to the left onto the beach.

Caution: Both lights are on private property.

 Cabot Beach Provincial Park

The original light on Fish Island, located offshore and now decommissioned, was nearly destroyed by a violent storm. The light was replaced with a steel tower and the original wooden structure was moved to Cabot Beach Provincial Park. No longer in official use, the light has been given a weathered look and is used as a prop in filming the TV series Emily of New Moon.

Directions: Cabot Beach Provincial Park is off Route 20, north of Malpeque. In the day-use (beach) portion of the park, the light tower is located near the shoreline.

5. Ship to Shore

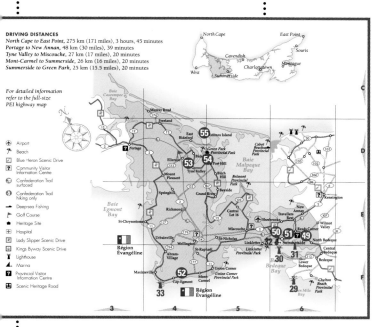

DRIVING DISTANCES
North Cape to East Point, 275 km (171 miles), 3 hours, 45 minutes
Portage to New Annan, 48 km (30 miles), 39 minutes
Tyne Valley to Miscouche, 27 km (17 miles), 20 minutes
Mont-Carmel to Summerside, 26 km (16 miles), 20 minutes
Summerside to Green Park, 25 km (15.5 miles), 20 minutes

*For detailed information
refer to the full-size
PEI highway map*

- ✈ Airport
- 🏖 Beach
- Blue Heron Scenic Drive
- ? Community Visitor Information Centre
- Confederation Trail surfaced
- Confederation Trail hiking only
- Deepsea Fishing
- Golf Course
- Heritage Site
- Hospital
- Lady Slipper Scenic Drive
- Kings Byway Scenic Drive
- Lighthouse
- Marina
- ? Provincial Visitor Information Centre
- Scenic Heritage Road

● Adventures

49 The Island Way Farm B&B
50 Spinnaker's Landing
51 College of Piping
52 The Bottle Houses
53 Tyne Valley
54 Green Park Shipbuilding Museum
55 Lennox Island

🏮 Lighthouses

29 Indian Head
30 Summerside Front Range
31 Summerside Range
32 Summerside Outer Range
33 Cap-Egmont

Ship to Shore: Introduction

Historically, shipbuilding has been important to the western region of Prince Edward Island, where impressive wooden sailing vessels were constructed and set out to travel to ports around the world. Today, the region celebrates its seafaring heritage. From Green Park, which honours the days of

"wooden ships and iron men," to the glass houses at Cap-Egmont—built by Edouard Arsenault, a retired lighthouse keeper—maritime traditions are honoured in museums, with festivals, and in the refined architecture of Summerside homes that recall the prosperous days of the Age of Sail in the 1800s.

Where the past and present join.

Keeping watch in Summerside Harbour.

Summerside, Canada's newest city as of April 1995, also prospered with the silver fox breeding industry in the early 1900s, and elegant homes

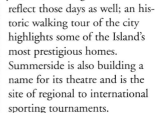

reflect those days as well; an historic walking tour of the city highlights some of the Island's most prestigious homes. Summerside is also building a name for its theatre and is the site of regional to international sporting tournaments.

West of Summerside is La Région Evangéline, where the Island's Acadian heritage and culture over three centuries is evident in place names such as Miscouche and Cap-Egmont, and the lively Acadian festivals and events such as Festival Acadien, held throughout the summer.

Of course, picturesque communities and scenic coastal vistas, like those found at Malpeque Bay, abound in the Ship to Shore region. No DayTour region around the Island suffers from a scarcity of natural beauty or maritime charm.

The Island Way Farm Bed and Breakfast

One of the best ways to experience the "real" Prince Edward Island is to spend time with the people who live there. A farm stay is a popular alternative to traditional accommodations because it exposes guests to a genuine Island atmosphere amid hospitable residents. The province has always had a strong agricultural component to its economy, and to spend a night or more on a working farm is a great way to experience what this unique lifestyle is all about. If guests desire, they may visit the barns, pet the animals, and explore trails through the fields.

Route 1A near
Summerside
tel. (902)436-7405
or 1-800-361-3435
Seasonal

The Island Way Farm Bed and Breakfast, just outside Summerside, is one of a number of farm properties that welcomes guests during the summer months. An active 81-ha (200-acre) grain and potato farm, it features a lovely large 1910 farmhouse. With four bedrooms and two private baths, owners Ruth Anne and Gordon Waugh offer an hospitable glimpse into rural Island life.

Guests can go horseback riding or cycling on surrounding country roads. Some of the trained horses in the farm's stable have been featured in the TV series *Emily of New Moon* as well as other productions. This bed and breakfast also has walking trails through the fields and along the pretty Wilmot River. Enjoying the countryside and leisure activities are part of the appeal at the Island Way Farm Bed and Breakfast.

Jennifer Waugh and friend.

The Island Way Farm B&B.

Adventure

Travel 28 km (17 mi.) from Confederation Bridge on Route 11 tel. (902)436-6692 or (902)436-2246 (in winter)
Some operations are seasonal.

Hospitality is key in Summerside and it shows as you walk along friendly streets that boast some of the finest examples of traditional architecture on the Island. The Age of Sail provided enough wealth for shipbuilders and owners to build stately homes. Fox farming, which was one of the most profitable industries early in this century, was the other source of wealth that supported such elaborate homes. The local Visitor Information Centre has ample and interesting details on an historic walking tour of the city that highlights the striking architecture of these impressive houses.

The renovated waterfront—highlighted by Spinnaker's Landing, a unique shopping and enter-

tainment area—is the pride of Summerside. Children will especially love the large boat playground while adults enjoy a variety of shops along the boardwalk. Even if time doesn't permit taking in a performance at the Jubilee Theatre next door, a

Children's play area.

stroll along Bedeque Bay is relaxing and pleasant. Visit the Lighthouse Look-out, the Saturday morning Farmer's Market, the boat shed filled with dis-

The shops of Spinnaker's Landing.

plays and videos about traditional boat-building methods and the Island's fishing heritage, or perhaps take a boat tour.

Be sure to partake in a meal at Seasons in Thyme restaurant on Water Street. The food is superb, the service excellent.

Free

College of Piping

Perhaps the most compelling reason to visit the only year-round college of Celtic performing arts in North America is for the music. While the College of Piping offers a wide variety of courses in playing bagpipes, drumming, Highland dancing, step-dancing, fiddling, and Gaelic singing, it also has an extensive program of performances.

During the summer, while visitors tour the facilities, they may also observe students at work; often they will oblige with an impromptu demonstration. For those with a desire to learn more about Celtic music and dance, there are summertime workshops available. Registration is required.

Every Monday to Thursday evening in the summer the college hosts a ceilidh on the fully covered main stage. These lively, traditional concerts of music and dance are open to the public for a small fee, offering great insight into the Scottish heritage that is part of the Island's heritage, too.

619 Water Street East, Summerside
tel. (902)436-5377 or toll free 1-877-224-7473
Open year-round
www.piping.pe.ca

Celebrating Celtic traditions.

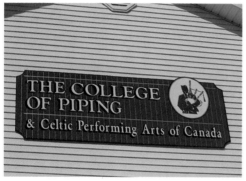

The college is also involved in the annual Summerside Highland Gathering and Military Tattoo, usually held at the end of June. In addition, there is a concert series throughout the season, featuring well-known performing artists from the Atlantic Provinces.

Free

Route 11 at
Cap-Egmont
tel. (902)854-2987 or
(902)854-2254 (off-
season)
Seasonal

Edouard Arsenault of Cap-Egmont was a lobster fisherman, carpenter, and boat-builder. An early, perhaps inadvertent, advocate of recycling, he also helped to preserve history and develop tourism in the region. After retiring as the last resident keeper of Cap-Egmont lighthouse (a short distance west along Route 11), he began, in 1980, to construct buildings made of glass bottles. Using liquor and wine bottles, and working from plans set down only in his sixty-five-year-old imagination, he created three small buildings from more than twenty-five thousand bottles.

Still kept open to the public by his daughter, Réjeanne, the structures have been completely reno-vated amidst her father's beautiful flower gardens. Visitors may enter these buildings, which create a vari-coloured lustre when the sun shines through the glass walls. The chapel is perhaps the most interesting creation, with pews also made of glass bottles. One of the few shops on the Island to sell T-shirts printed in French is on site, and there is an attractive open area near the ocean.

A glassy attraction.

"A true labour of love that lives on in the minds of all those who enter." P.C.

$

Tyne Valley

A meandering river, edged in rich green lawns and low hanging trees, flows through the centre of the pastoral little hamlet called Tyne Valley. A charming combination of past and present, one of Prince Edward Island's prettiest communities is a quiet stop to appreciate what some of the spots off the beaten path have to offer in natural beauty and local talent.

On Route 178
tel. (902)831-2191 (for theatre tickets)
Seasonal

Handcrafted "Shoreline" woollen sweaters, created by Lesley Dubey, can be found at the Tyne Valley Studio Art Gallery along with work by other Island artists. Tyne Valley is also home to the historic Brittania Hall Theatre, which offers local productions and musical concerts. One of the Island's fine bed and breakfasts is located here. The Doctor's Inn, a nineteenth-century village home, is open year-round. This community also hosts the Tyne Valley Oyster Festival, featuring famous Malpeque oysters. Discover a lovely setting and the tranquillity that are characteristic of Prince Edward Island.

A tranquil river in Tyne Valley.

Green Park
Shipbuilding Museum

Port Hill, Route 12
tel. (902)831-7947
Seasonal
www.metamedia.pe.
ca/peimuseum

Shipbuilding was a major Island industry in the nineteenth century. The Green Park Shipbuilding Museum invites visitors to experience that prosperous, exciting Age of Sail. While the Interpretive Centre has a number of displays, including ship rigs and knot-tying, the property outside is most enjoyable. A footpath leads across an open field, past the carpenter and blacksmith shops, to the re-created shipyard that is typical of the almost two hundred shipyards that drove the economy of the province during the 1800s. The beginning of a 200-ton brigantine is under construction, with the keel and stern laid near the water's edge. The stem and ribs, or frame, are piled nearby.

"The Age of Sail" comes alive at Green Park.

Nestled among the trees beyond the Interpretive Centre is the Yeo House, formerly owned by James Yeo Jr. Open to the public—but not wheelchair accessible—this house was constructed in the luxurious Victorian style and is a typical 1860s home of a wealthy ship owner.

Green Park has several walking trails and offers a variety of daytime and evening activities, such as lectures, concerts, ghost storytelling, and festivals.

$

Lennox Island

Lennox Island, joined to Prince Edward Island by a causeway, juts out into picturesque Malpeque Bay. This native community is home to two spots that are well worth the slight diversion: Micmac Productions and Indian Art and Craft of North America. Aboriginal legends and heritage are represented among the fine artistic works at these two locations.

Micmac Productions, the only manufacturer of fine Mi'kmaq earthenware figurines in Canada, is located in a small building in the centre of the village, near the school and church. Free tours are offered year-round (Monday to Friday) of the production of the Glooscap Legends Collection: eight numbered figurines that depict climactic moments in the life of Mi'kmaq hero Glooscap. According to tradition, Glooscap was chosen to carry a piece of heaven to earth to create a Mi'kmaq homeland. This legend became the first, titled "the Gift," in the figurine series.

Not far from Micmac Productions is a fine handcrafts shop, Indian Art and Craft of North Amercia. Open seasonally, or off-season by chance or appointment, the shop specializes in ash splint baskets. There are traditional and non-traditional pieces, such as beadwork, carvings, and pottery. Books and stationery are also sold here. A screened-in porch and picnic tables overlook Malpeque Bay. Together, the shops are a haven of aboriginal art and culture.

Route 163, off Route 12
Micmac Productions: tel. (902)831-2277
Open year-round
www.peisland.com/micmac/legends.htm
Indian Art and Craft of North America:
Route 163, off Route 12
tel. (902)831-2653
www.peisland.com/micmac/crafts.htm

Indian Arts and Crafts of North America: Aboriginal art and culture.

Free

29 | **Indian Head ***

The drive out to Indian Head at MacCallums Point will take a few minutes, but the view is breathtaking from this interesting octagon tower atop an octagon building that appears to grow out of the solid concrete base and is used to support this most unusual modern design structure. Situated at the outer end of a long stone breakwater, the light is in the middle of Summerside Harbour entrance, as if in defiance of the winds and sea. At low tide visitors can walk almost to the light via a sandbar. Walking or climbing along the breakwater is dangerous because of large slippery rocks, and if the tide happens to be rolling in. The light is also visible across the harbour from Summerside and looks quite different from this vantage point.

Directions: At the intersection of Routes 171 and 112 in Bedeque, follow Route 112 for a distance of 9 km (5.6 mi.) to the end. (The pavement changes to a dirt road at 5.7 km or 3.5 mi.) There is a small parking and turning space atop the low cliff overlooking the water.

Indian Head.

29 | **Summerside Front Range (Decommissioned Light)**

Summerside Front Range.

On the way to Indian Head the decommissioned Summerside front range is visible on the left from the road. Originally located on the wharf in Summerside, it was later moved to this location on private property. (The front range in Summerside was rebuilt as a skeleton tower. See the next listing.) Permission should be obtained before walking to the light. This structure is an excellent example of how a former light has been privately preserved and is now used as a summer home while maintaining the integrity of the original design.

Directions: At the intersection of Routes 171 and 112 in Bedeque, follow Route 112 a distance of 8 km (5 mi.) towards Indian Head lighthouse. (The pavement ends after 5.7 km or 3.5 mi.) The light will be visible through the trees to the left. A narrow road leads to the property.

Summerside Range

The front range now in Summerside is a skeleton tower near the outer end of the Summerside wharf. The rear range is 20 m (65 ft.) tall with a tapered base leading to a square upper tower. The resulting design is unique in Prince Edward Island, especially with the wide base in proportion to the small top and the tiny square lantern. Located next to the street, it is a striking structure.

Directions: To get to the rear range, follow the road marked Glovers Shore off Route 11 (Water Street), on the east side of the city. The light is on private property beside the road. Parking and turning are limited.

Caution: Private property.

Summerside Rear Range.

Summerside Outer Range

Both front and rear range lights are easy to locate and are the traditional pepper-shaker design. Both have a white upper portion and an attached red vertical day marker. Identical in design with a flared support under the platform, these lights are highly accessible. By examining the positioning of these towers it is easy to understand how the range light system works. The Indian Head light may be viewed in the distance situated in the middle of the harbour entrance.

Directions: Follow Route 11 (Water Street), on the west side of Summerside. The rear light is situated beside the highway. The front light is accessible by turning off Route 11 on MacKenzie Road and driving a distance of 300 m (330 yds.). The front range light will be on the left, beside the road.

Caution: No off-street parking available.

Summerside Outer Front Range.

Cap-Egmont *

First put into service on September 1, 1884, the Cap-Egmont lighthouse has guided many vessels through the Northumberland Strait beyond Egmont and Bedeque Bays. This square tapered light station is capped with a red octagon lantern and sits high upon the cape. The last keeper of the light, the late Edouard Arsenault, is famous locally as the creator of the bottle houses. On a clear day a glimpse of the New Brunswick coastline may be visible on the horizon.

Directions: Off Route 11, west of Cap-Egmont village, turn into the road leading to the Cap-Egmont wharf (Fishing Cove Harbour) and then immediately turn left onto a narrow dirt lane. There is parking and turning space in the open field near the lighthouse. The light may also be seen, at a distance, from the Cap-Egmont wharf.

Cap-Egmont.

Caution: Narrow lane; steep cliffs without fences.

6. North by Northwest

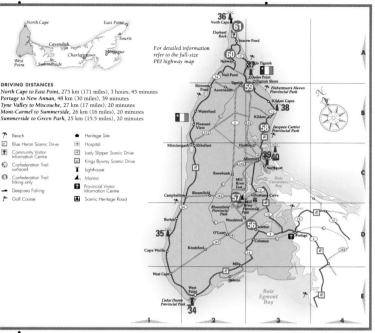

DRIVING DISTANCES
North Cape to East Point, 275 km (171 miles), 3 hours, 45 minutes
Portage to New Annan, 48 km (30 miles), 39 minutes
Tyne Valley to Miscouche, 27 km (17 miles), 20 minutes
Mont-Carmel to Summerside, 26 km (16 miles), 20 minutes
Summerside to Green Park, 25 km (15.5 miles), 20 minutes

🏖 Beach
📘 Blue Heron Scenic Drive
❓ Community Visitor Information Centre
🚲 Confederation Trail surfaced
🚲 Confederation Trail hiking only
➤ Deep-sea Fishing
🏌 Golf Course

🏛 Heritage Site
✚ Hospital
📙 Lady Slipper Scenic Drive
📗 Kings Byway Scenic Drive
🏛 Lighthouse
⚓ Marina
❓ Provincial Visitor Information Centre
📕 Scenic Heritage Road

● **Adventures**

56 MacAusland's Woollen Mill

57 Rodd Mill River Resort and Aquaplex

58 Jacques Cartier and Cedar Dunes Provincial Parks

59 Confederation Trail, Tignish

60 Elephant Rock

61 North Cape

🏛 **Lighthouses**

34 West Point

35 Howards Cove

36 North Cape

37 Big Tignish

38 Miminegash Rear Range

39 Northport Range

40 Cascumpec

Perhaps the greatest appeal for this northwest region of Prince Edward Island is that life is much the same as it has been for generations. The rich red soil continues to support farms and the deep blue sea continues to support the fisheries, two central pillars of the local villages. Known to residents as "West Prince," the north by northwest region is noted for its red sandstone cliffs and sand beaches—hallmarks of the province.

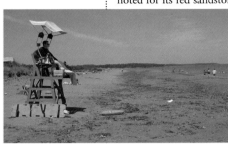

Moving to a slower beat.

There are numerous provincial parks in this DayTour area. Mill River Provincial Park features one of the Island's top 18-hole golf courses, a resort hotel, and seemingly endless recreational activities from racquet sports to water sports. Cedar Dunes Provincial Park has a spectacular sand beach, and Jacques Cartier Provincial Park marks the site where it is believed the French explorer landed in 1534.

Visitors to the region will find notable communities and naturally occurring landmarks. For instance, Alberton's claim to fame is that the silver fox industry began there. Tignish, with Acadian and Irish heritage, is home to Canada's first fisheries co-op, which still operates today. Near North Cape is Elephant Rock—a magnificent sandstone formation, sculpted by winds and tides, that strongly resembled its namesake until it recently "lost its trunk."

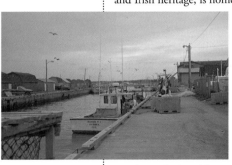

The Harbour at Judes Point.

Homage to economic staples is paid at such places as the Potato Museum at O'Leary and the Irish Moss Interpretive Centre at Miminegash. You can learn how the humble potato is as vital to the Island as wheat is to western Canada, or sample seaweed pie at the interpretive centre.

Wherever you journey in the north by northwest region, you'll glimpse Island heritage and tradition, unadulterated beauty, and a pace that infuses the notion of "vacation" with meaning.

MacAusland's Woollen Mill

Adventure

This family business has been in existence since 1932. Visitors to MacAusland's Woollen Mill are invited to view the production of yarn and blankets and ask questions of the friendly staff. The whole process of carding, spinning, and weaving wool into yarn and the famous MacAusland blankets takes place inside the modest wooden building. The equipment was once powered by the nearby waterfall but is now electrically run. It is interesting to see how the sheep's wool is washed, dried, and cleaned before carding (combing) and spinning into threads to produce yarn. In a separate operation to make blankets, the threads are woven on a loom, pre-shrunk, washed, dyed, brushed, cut, and hemmed into a finished product.

Outside, there is a small dam and waterfall. Next door to the mill is the Old Mill Craft Company, which is seasonally operated as an arts and crafts shop. The mill bills itself as the only producer in Atlantic Canada of 100 per cent pure virgin wool blankets. Visitors may purchase yarn or blankets on site.

Route 2, close to Mill River Provincial Park
tel. (902)859-3005
Open year round
(Monday to Friday)

MacAusland's Woollen Mill—where tradition is still important.

Free

Rodd Mill River Resort and Aquaplex

Located in Mill River
Provincial Park
tel. (902)859-3555 or
1-800-565-7633
Seasonal

For accommodations, dining, golf, and aquatic fun all rolled into one beautiful setting, Rodd Mill River Resort is the answer. Situated in Mill River Provincial Park, the resort overlooks an 18-hole championship golf course. The main dining room provides delicious meals at moderate prices and offers a great view of the course. This casual licensed facility features a menu to please almost any palate and includes a children's menu.

The highlight of the resort is the aquaplex (a great alternative on rainy days) with an indoor 25-m (82-ft.) swimming pool, waterslide, whirlpool, and sauna. Two squash courts and a Nautilus exercise room are available. Tennis courts are on site, and a pleasing variety of recreational activities can be arranged, such as canoeing, windsurfing, and cycling.

The resort life at Mill River—overlooking the golf course.

The resort offers a wide range of discounts and vacation packages, including "kids eat free" during July and August, and free breakfast for seniors in the low season. Non-smoking suites and double rooms are available in the three-storey hotel. Although the resort caters to summer season visitors, it re-opens during the winter for cross-country skiing and other snow-based activities.

Jacques Cartier and Cedar Dunes Provincial Parks

Prince Edward Island is renowned for its red or white sand beaches and warm water. Naturally, then, some beaches may be crowded during the summer peak of July and August. To enjoy a less crowded beach, visit one of the Island's provincial parks.

Jacques Cartier Provincial Park, for instance, honours the Island's first European visitor and celebrates the event of his landing with an annual Rediscovery Day each July. A full-time naturalist arranges nature walks and programs for children. The beautiful Gulf of St. Lawrence beach is supervised in summer. At low tide, the beach runs, unbroken, from the park to North Cape. There is also a 9-ha (22-acre) campground with related services, such as a laundromat and canteen. A fee is charged for camping.

Cedar Dunes Provincial Park, on the opposite side of the Island, is another fine choice and partly wheelchair accessible. There is an exceptional white sand beach along the Northumberland Strait, reportedly the "warmest waters north of the

Jacques Cartier
Provincial Park:
Route 12, east of
Alberton
tel. (902)853-8632
Seasonal
Cedar Dunes
Provincial Park:
Route 14, south of
O'Leary
tel. (902)859-8785 or
(902)859-8790 (in
winter)
Seasonal

Jacques Cartier
Provincial Park.

Carolinas." The supervised beach stretches for several kilometres. Nature walks are arranged by park naturalists. The park also has a 40-ha (100-acre) campground. A fee is charged for camping. The unique West Point lighthouse, which has been converted to a charming inn, is on site. (See page 93 in the Lighthouses section.)

Free

Western end of
route 2
tel. 1-800-463-4734
(902) 463-4734 (on
PEI) for
Confederation Trail
information
Open year-round

The small community of Tignish was the end of the line for the former Prince Edward Island railway line. Since Canadian National Railways closed out all the rail lines in the province, much of the old roadbed has been converted into the Confederation Trail. Ideal for both hiking and biking, the wide trail is almost flat and has a rolled stone dust surface. It runs, in stages, between Elmira and Tignish, offering a scenic, safe route for those who prefer to avoid the highways.

Tignish considers itself Mile 0, leading to what may be a complete 350-km (217-mi.) trail that crosses the Island. Elmira, on the opposite end of the Island, also claims to be Mile 0, so it appears the trail has two beginnings and no end.

Hike and bike the
Confederation Trail.

Confederation Trail may be accessed on foot or bicycle at a number of points, including the community of Tignish. There is a nice little fence and gateway that mark the beginning of the trail system here. There is ample parking nearby. A map, though not necessary to navigate the trail, is available from any Visitor Information Centre, and it does indicate where to find food services, washroom facilities, and trail shelters.

Free

Elephant Rock

The action of the tides and wind have created an unusual natural attraction near North Cape. Elephant Rock looked just like a large pachyderm standing quietly on the beach, filling his large trunk in the Northumberland Strait until it recently lost its trunk. The grass atop its "back" looks much like a howdah, a seat for riders, awaiting the driver or mahout.

Elephant Rock may be seen from several points atop the steep cliff although care should be exercised along the edge. A rough path has been cut down to the beach on the north side. Once on the beach, at low tide it is possible to walk to the rock, which gives a new appreciation for its impressive size.

The well-marked drive to the area is only a few minutes from Route 12. Since the site hasn't been

Off Route 12, near
Seacow Pond
tel. 1-800-565-2299
(West Prince
Tourism Association)
Open year-round

developed, there are no facilities, except for parking in an area cut out of the field atop the cliff. Drivers should note that in the vicinity of Elephant Rock the dirt road becomes narrow and is close to the cliff edge. (Also, in wet weather, this road might become quite muddy.) A panoramic ocean vista awaits.

An odd rock on the beach.

Free 👪 📷

North Cape

At the end of
Route 12
tel. 1-800-565-2299
(West Prince
Tourism Association)
Seasonal

At one time, the sole structure at North Cape was the first generation style lighthouse. The light still stands but the area is shared now with a wind testing station, an interpretive centre, and a fine restaurant, which offers some of the most spectacular scenery on the Island.

North Cape overlooks one of the world's longest natural rock reefs, which separates the Northumberland Strait and the Gulf of St. Lawrence. At low tide, visitors can walk along part of the reef to see seabirds and other examples of marine life.

Due to the constant wind, North Point was selected for the testing of wind turbines, which can be seen from behind a fenced area. A video about the test site may be viewed in the interpretive centre, which also has a gift shop and restaurant.

In the interpretive centre, visitors can collect an "I visited North Cape" ribbon, which they can redeem at the East Point gift shop for a Tip-to-Tip Traveller's Award certificate. (Or, if an East Point ribbon has already been collected, request the certificate here.)

North Cape—
land's end.

Free 🏛 📷

West Point *

The West Point light, at the southwestern tip of the province, is unique in several ways. First, it is one of the few that has wide black and white horizontal stripes. Second, although still operational as a Coast Guard light, it has been converted into an inn, which includes nine guest rooms in total, some in the tower and some in the attached former keeper's quarters. Third, it is the tallest light of square design in the province

Constructed in 1875, the 21-m (68-ft.) square tapered tower is 20 m (65 ft.) above the water near the sandy beach of Cedar Dunes Provincial Park. The light was automated in 1963. The lighthouse has photographs and displays depicting the light-keeping heritage. (There is a small admission for

West Point.

the museum and to climb to the top of the lantern for a spectacular view.) Perhaps you will glimpse the legendary "Phantom Ship" as it drifts ablaze through the night.

Directions: In West Point on Route 14, follow signs for Cedar Dunes Provincial Park. The light station is just past the park entrance and is well marked. There is a parking lot close to the light.

35 Howards Cove

This 6-m (19-ft.) white tower is situated on a hill near the fishing harbour of Seal Point. It is operated seasonally. Although the light is somewhat insignificant in terms of lighthouses on the Island (it is not shown on the highway map), the area provides a good view point for observing coastal community life in Prince Edward Island. The Acadian region surrounding this point is rich in French heritage.

Directions: From Route 14 near Howards Cove, follow the road to Seal Point. The light is on a hill.

Caution: Foghorn.

36 North Cape *

North Cape.

Situated at the northernmost tip of Prince Edward Island, the traditional white octagon tower is located close to an interpretation centre and wind test site. It is often considered the most important light station on the Island as it warns ships to beware of the 1.5 km (1 mi.) long natural rock reef—one of the longest in the world—that projects out from the rough escarpment of North Cape. Built in 1866 the 19-m (63-ft.) lighthouse has been automated (like all the lighthouses in the province). The light and a communications tower are now enclosed by fencing.

Directions: Follow Route 12, which ends at North Cape. Parking and turning space are located near the lighthouse.

Caution: Steep cliffs.

Big Tignish
(Decommissioned Light)

This small white tower is situated on the edge of the "run" that allows fishing boats to enter the protected harbour of Judes Point. Although the light is decommissioned and somewhat in disrepair, its location on the side of the "run" is striking. It is a perfect example of how modern technology has made such local lights obsolete. In spite of constant changes, this little light station has become an intricate part of the fishing community. Like many other similar structures, its removal would not only make the area less picturesque but would be destroying a vital part of the seafaring heritage of the region.

Directions: On Route 12, just south of the intersection with Route 2, take the paved road eastward towards Judes Point and Tignish Shore. At 1.2 km (0.7 mi.) turn left (at the Royal Star Foods Ltd. plant) and follow the road for 0.8 km (0.5 mi.) to the light, which is at the entrance to the harbour, just past the fish plant. A small parking and turning space are near the light.

Big Tignish.

Caution: Road narrows near the lighthouse; entrance to harbour ("run") has no railings.

Miminegash Rear Range
(Decommissioned Light)

Beside Route 12 at Cape Kildare is a small light, which was initially used as a range light. It is believed that this originally was the rear range at Miminegash, and it was transported to this location. It was probably of the type for which the keeper lit the lantern and hoisted it up into position. Situated on private property, the range light is visible beside the highway.

Directions: Follow Route 12 at Cape Kildare. The light is on the eastern side of highway.

Caution: No off-road parking; private property.

Miminegash Rear Range.

Northport Range *

The front range is a skeleton tower near the outer end of the old railway wharf. The rear range is a white tower with a tapered bottom and straight-sided top section. Similar to the unique design of

the Summerside Rear Range, only shorter, the lantern is white with red corners and a vertical day stripe has been painted down the front of the structure. Its location beside the roadway allows for closer examination and its picturesque location beside the water makes it worth the side trip to visit.

Directions: Off Route 12 in Alberton, follow the highway to Northport. The rear range will be on the left, beside the main road and just past the Historic Sea

Northport Rear Range.

Rescue Station. The front range is a skeleton tower erected on the nearby former railway dock.

Cascumpec (Decommissioned Light, Off Shore)

This former offshore light station hugs the shore of a low-lying island. The tapered tower is attached to

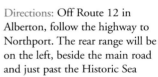

the keeper's house, which is now privately owned.
A new steel light tower with an enclosed centre stairway has been erected near the original light. The traditional style lighthouse, reminiscent of an isolated lifestyle for the keeper and his family, is in stark contrast to the modern structure erected beside it.

Cascumpec.

This is the only off-shore lightstation visible from Prince Edward Island and is part of a tradition of dedicated lightkeeping that has been the mainstay of the protection offered by the building of lighthouses.

Directions: Off Route 12 in Alberton, follow the highway to Northport. The former light station will be visible on the left, near the Historic Sea Rescue Station.

Index: Adventure

Index: Lighthouses